The

Presence,
Power *and*
Heart *of* God

Partnering in His Ministry

Randy Fisk

The Presence, Power and Heart of God –
Partnering in His Ministry
Copyright © 2006 by Randy Fisk

Published by ByronArts, Northwoods, Illinois 60185
SAN 850-0517   www.ByronArts.com

ISBN: 0-9777226-0-0

For inquiries about the book or availability to come and teach, the author may be contacted at Randy.Fisk@ByronArts.com.

Edited by Ginny Emery and France Marcott

Printed in the United States of America

Dedicated to my wife, Mary—
my love and my joy

Acknowledgments

I would like to thank Mary, my wonderful wife and partner in life and ministry, for her help and encouragement in writing this book. And I would also like to thank my amazing children, Holly, Becky and Mandy, for who they are and the inspiration they are to me. They will go far in the Lord. I also deeply appreciate my many friends, colleagues and fabulous pastors with whom I discovered more and more of God. Many thanks to France Marcott and all who helped with the editing of this book. And I am so grateful to my friend and editor, Ginny Emery, for her many contributions and for the wealth of knowledge I learned from her. I also want to express my deep gratitude to my good friend George Koch, without whose love, encouragement and support this book would not have been written. Finally, I would like to thank my Lord and God who always gives me more than I ask. I love You, everything You are and all that You do.

Contents

Forward

Church of the Resurrection has always loved to pray. When I was first interviewed for the position of Pastor, the discussions finished much earlier than anyone had anticipated. Someone looked up at the clock and said, "Hey—we have a little extra time. Let's go upstairs and pray!" This was met with an immediate and enthusiastic response from all present. How odd, I thought, a church that *loves* to pray. It wasn't heavy with obligation, instead it was like the anticipation of seeing an old friend.

We all went to the sanctuary, stood around the altar, held hands, and prayed. And my Lord could they pray! Confident, heartfelt, intimate, at home with Jesus and talking to him with passion! I was stunned, impressed and thrilled! I was offered the job, and took it with delight. What a place to be a pastor!

As our time together there unfolded, at some point we realized that we all loved praying, but we didn't know nearly as much about prayer as we desired: maybe we could learn to pray even better. The disciples had the same desire, and when they asked Jesus to teach them to pray, he gave them the Lord's Prayer. Maybe we could grow in prayer, too. We set off on an adventure to learn how: in many books, churches, conferences and places of prayer. We continue to do this.

A couple of our members learned about a class being taught at a nearby Vineyard church, all about prayer, and healing, and ministering in teams. When they began attending, they came back with rave reports on how much they were learning and seeing. They said the teacher was wonderful, insightful and they were learning new things. They treasured what he was teaching them, and the quiet manner he had, along with the power of prayer that he taught and demonstrated. His name was Randy Fisk.

I asked them to invite him to teach at our church—a liturgical, Anglican (Episcopal) church that a lot of Vineyard folks might imagine to be stiff and ritualistic. I thought he would be wary. But he readily agreed, and shortly thereafter the classes began at Resurrection. I liked Randy immediately. He was indeed unassuming, gentle, and also very bright. His presentations were eye-opening, clear and biblically sound— and always ready for whatever Jesus wanted to do with us.

Jesus did a lot, right there in our midst.

Randy took us more deeply into prayer, and in understanding what it is (and isn't), and how to pray immediately, and how to work shoulder-to-shoulder in *teams*—to minister to each other and to those God sends our way. We learned so much, and it became so much a part of us, that it is hard now to remember how we prayed before.

Now there was a revolutionary aspect to it: we *gathered* to pray, as *teams*, and the Holy Spirit swept through us and around us as we prayed. Randy called it "the dancing hand of God," and we saw it at work, directing first this person, then another. There were no "superstar" prayer ministers, but the gathered priesthood of believers, at work together, ministering healing and hope and being astonished by the wonders God did as we prayed.

Jesus was there. Anything could happen. And did.

Randy began assembling these teachings into a book, and we began pushing him hard to complete it and get it out for the whole church. We didn't want to keep it just for ourselves! This is that book, and it can begin a profound adventure for those who love God and love to pray, and want more of both. It can revolutionize the prayer of the local church, and it will do just that if you let it. I commend it to you for your joy.

The Rev Dr George Byron Koch
Church of the Resurrection
West Chicago, IL 60185
www.resurrection.org

Introduction

The Presence, Power and Heart of God – Partnering in His Ministry is about equipping people to minister effectively, especially as they work together in teams. Yet, it is about more than that. It touches upon the ministry of all believers and their God-given desire to take part in the greatest privilege imaginable: to walk close to their God and to see Him impact the lives of others. It touches on the journey every believer is destined and called to walk. It even touches on the magnificent journey of the Church itself, which may be on the verge of a reformation in the way and place we think ministry happens.

The ministry I am about to describe is not the concept of "being in the ministry" as most people think of it. Rather, I am talking about the type of activity that Jesus did as He ministered to individuals, doing what He saw the Father doing. He said this ministry is for us, too, (John 14:12) and promised that when two or three of us ask Him for anything He will do it, for He Himself will be among us (Matt. 18:19-20). It is experiencing God at work—and His presence, power and heart coming into situations where people desperately need Him.

A portion of this book is about healing, but healing is only one of the things this ministry is about. This ministry extends the arms of the church to bring the healing, encouragement, nurturing, words, empowerment and individual attention that Jesus wants to give to every member of His flock. I believe this ministry is also poised to play a significant role in the front-line work of expanding God's kingdom—in homes and at the marketplace—not only within the four walls of the church.

God is giving His people a deep desire to come close to Him and become equipped and used in effective ministry. This desire is being felt by people from all across the Body of Christ. Many feel a sense of urgency to answer this call.

I believe several factors are behind this sense of urgency. First, social maladies like abuse, neglect and drug dependence are at epidemic proportions today and there is an overwhelming need for healing everywhere. Second, many are feeling that a great harvest is at our doorstep. When people start coming to faith in Jesus in large numbers and turning to the churches, they will need to be healed, prayed for, encouraged and equipped. We must be ready. Third, I believe God is bringing about what some have called The Second Reformation: God placing ministry into the hands of the people, radically transforming church members from spectators to participants. This book is written for all who are hearing these calls.

In this book I share both a vision of reformation and my personal experiences in equipping ministry teams in the basics of healing, moving with the Holy Spirit and hearing His voice. While ministry teams are certainly not all that a second reformation is about, I believe they are a representative part of it. I could have written the book from the perspective of equipping individuals to minister—that certainly fits in with the vision of the Second Reformation. But I think it is far more important to discuss how we can work together as teams, supporting one another, being used together by the Holy Spirit and flowing with each other in both unity and diversity. Although one can put a thousand to flight, two can put ten thousand to flight. This is truly at the heart of the Second Reformation.

Such a reformation may change the expression of the church as we know it. All agree that the church is about people, not buildings. However, many have become so accustomed to thinking that the activity of the church is within the church building that any other view seems foreign. In the Bible, however, almost all of the supernatural acts of God were not done within the four walls of a church or temple, but in the every-day world. When the ministry of God comes into the hands of the people who already live and work in that world, we will once again see the ministry of Jesus out in the highways and byways—the same place He sent His disciples two by two—where again He will send His empowered teams.

Just as there are many types of Spiritual gifts, so, too, the team members and even the teams themselves will be different. Some will specialize in healing, some in servanthood, some in music. Some will be specifically called for special assignments. All will be empowered and bring the Kingdom of God to a world in desperate need of it.

Although I discuss specific issues and give many valuable helps related to equipping, my experience has been that the success of both ministry teams and individual team members depends far more on foundational heart attitudes than on knowing a lot of particulars or on having a prescribed level of giftedness. Therefore, a significant part of this book is about seeking and receiving the heart attitudes essential to effective ministry. This book also lays foundations in topics I have discovered to be vital to ministry: Who is the Holy Spirit? What are the deeper aspects of faith, grace and the gifts of the Holy Spirit and how are they used in ministering to others? How can we learn to listen to God? What is our ministerial relationship with God all about?

To some who are new to the idea that God speaks directly to and through people today, some of the tenets of this book may present a challenge. If that is you, I suggest some books that lay a solid Scriptural and practical foundation. Their references are given in the bibliography. For a foundation in the prophetic gifts, I would highly recommend Jack Deere's book *Surprised by the Voice of God*. It is thorough, scholarly, and fascinating reading. For a foundation in the Holy Spirit and how the presence of God can be experienced, I would recommend John White's book *When the Spirit Comes with Power*. It is rich in scholarship by someone who understands both the Word and people. Please read these books with a heart that is open to new ideas and willing to search the Scriptures to see for yourself.

Although you may have been exposed in the past to counterfeits and/or poor examples of healing and prophecy, the false and inadequate do not negate the true. I encourage you to check out for yourself the possibility that the Holy Spirit is still releasing His healing and prophetic gifts and that they can be, and even are, bringing the love of God in real, sensitive and powerful ways today. As always, go back to Jesus. What did He do?

My hope is that you will enjoy this book. Whether you glean a little or a lot from its pages, may you end up closer to the magnificent call on every believer's life to minister with the heart, style and power of God the Father, Son and Holy Spirit.

1
Beginnings of My Own Journey

My beginnings were fairly normal, if the word *normal* describes the antics of kids! If you were to take a snapshot from my childhood you might see me sweating in church one Sunday morning when I was eight years old. With every word the minister spoke, I sweat more and more profusely. It was not, unfortunately, because I was under the conviction of the Holy Spirit, but because I had worn my jeans and an old shirt underneath my Sunday clothes so I could make the fastest possible get-away to play. (Now there are churches where jeans and an old shirt *are* our Sunday clothes!) Memories of my early days in church were varied. I remember the elderly Mrs. Jordan complaining that yet again the minister had preached an entire sermon without talking about Jesus. I hadn't noticed. I remember a few years later that one family in the church called the police about another family in the church because they flew their flag upside down in protest of the Vietnam War. Although I was not very tuned in to the church scene, even at an early age I had an unusual hunger to know reality and had unfortunately concluded that church was not the answer. I did not know what was. I was convinced there was a God, but the lack of knowing much more than that left my hunger pushing me to seek who-knows-what for years of my life.

Towards the end of graduate school, I met Mary, the wonderful girl who became my wife. When she invited me to visit her church I was quick to agree. I would gladly hear the teachings about a "spiritual man," Jesus. That sounded like a cool thing to do. But on listening, I was struck for the first time that this "spiritual man" spoke words that would not allow one to sit on the fence. If He truly was spiritual and truthful, then I had to accept His claim that who He was and what He came to do were of epic importance. I had completely underestimated everything about Him. I would go home at night and read the Bible for hours on end, as if I were reading it for the first time.

About this time I attended a city-sponsored prayer breakfast. During this event, a young lady sang a very beautiful song about Jesus. I happened to notice Mary's pastor several tables away. As the young lady sang, tears rolled down his face. I have never told him this, but it shook me to the core. I had been searching for reality and found it not only in the staggering truth I was discovering, but also in the way it could impact a person's heart. The Lord was ambushing me on several different levels, and more ambushes were yet to come!

Through my pastor's impassioned sermons and broadcasts of Billy Graham crusades, I came to realize that God demanded far more than my acknowledgement of His truth. He wanted my life. He wanted me to hand over all my sin and nonsense, to walk into His arms, be forgiven and have everything made anew. So that is what I did, and that is what He did. It was beyond comparison with anything I had ever known or could have imagined.

The Lord began unveiling one new vista after another. At a large gathering of Christians, I heard, for the first time, of remarkable, present-day occurrences reminiscent of the Book of Acts—feeding the poor, miraculous healings, and heart-wrenching transformations of people's lives. It all sounded very familiar to me—I had just spent hours reading about such things in the Bible and wondering why I never heard about them in today's world. I was moved so deeply that I spent the majority of the weekend in tears. I remember saying to God that I would do anything to be in His Kingdom. If He wanted me to collect trash, it would be all right with me, as long as I could be a part of all this. After each session I would pick up discarded soda cans just to show Him I was serious. I would never be the same again.

The School of the First Reformation

About a year later, I felt an ever-increasing call in my heart to lay down what I was doing and pursue the ministry. My wife gave up her job, I left my position at a high-energy physics research facility, and we moved to St. Louis to attend a seminary of the Lutheran Church-Missouri Synod.

On the campus stood a bronze statue of Martin Luther. I loved to look at it, fascinated by the idea that he had brought reformation to the church. I used to wonder what would happen if he came back today. Would he be viewed as a hero or a rabble-rouser? Were it not for the five hundred years we have had to grow familiar with him, I suspected the latter.

Martin Luther taught that salvation comes from grace and not by our own efforts. He also did all he could to get the Scriptures into the hands of the people. In so doing, he fanned into flames a tremendous reformation that shook the church to its foundations.

> **In this second reformation ... *ministry* will come into the hands of the people.**

While at seminary, I came across writings that discussed the notion of a second reformation. In this second reformation, which is yet to come, *ministry* will come into the hands of the people. According to those who have studied the growth of the church, when the responsibility for the work of God is restricted to professionals, and the concerns and vision of

Christ are delegated to only a few, then the church at large can do little more than maintain the status quo. It cannot grow in the ways necessary to reach and disciple the entire world. Therefore it became obvious to me that this second reformation is not just an exciting idea; it is a critical necessity.

I was enthralled with the idea of reformation and especially this anticipated second reformation. The thought of every believer responding to the call upon him or her to minister was awesome to me. Years have passed, but the intensity with which this resonates within me has never worn off. The odd thing is that in the beginning, I had no idea what such a reformation would look like. I still don't know exactly, but I don't think that a single reformer like Luther will spearhead it. By its very nature, the second reformation must happen at the level of the individual "nameless" (i.e. known to God but not to man) believer, into whose hands ministry will fall. It will truly have to be a "God thing."

The God Squad

In time, God changed our direction once again and several years later we wound up in Northwestern Indiana, raising a wonderful family while I taught at Valparaiso University. Regarding church affiliation, however, I felt somewhat like a man without a country. I desired the sound, balanced theology of the Lutheran and evangelical churches, but also knew there was more of the presence and ministry of the Holy Spirit. I looked, but I could not find a denomination with both to the level I knew there could be.

About this time, one of my friends, Dave, discovered a series of tapes by John Wimber—a series based upon a course he taught at Fuller Seminary (*MC510: Signs, Wonders and Church Growth*). John Wimber, the founder of the Vineyard church movement, has impacted much of the church through heart-felt worship, a sensitive, powerful approach to healing, and, amazingly, an appreciation for sound Biblical theology and for the ministry of the Holy Spirit. Suddenly I found out that the country I had been longing for really existed. (I realize now that many churches and church movements emphasize both sound theology and the Holy Spirit.)

Dave, another friend and I became engrossed in these tapes. They began to satisfy a longing we had felt for years. As we passed tapes back and forth between us, oohing over the "good stuff" in them, we began to look like "tape junkies" to others in the church—and even to our wives! As John Wimber talked about praying for people to be healed, he had my complete attention; I had always longed to see healing. I had seen people pray for others to be healed, but had never imagined that I myself would ever be able to pray and see people healed. For years I had said to myself, if this ever happens to me, I'm going to show other people how to do it. But I really didn't think it would ever happen. The thought that I might be on the verge of seeing it happen was just too good!

The more we listened, the more excited we became. Eventually we said, "We just have to do this. We have to find some sick people!" I think our greatest fear in those days was not that people wouldn't be healed, but that we wouldn't be able to find any sick people to pray for! If any of us heard about a sick person, we'd get on the phone with each other and say, trying to restrain our excitement, "I just heard about a sick person. Let's go pray!" We'd jump in our cars and converge on that unsuspecting person. They got a visit from the "God Squad!" We'd pray, lay our hands on them and do whatever we thought we should do. God was amazingly faithful in showing us the way. What we lacked in finesse we made up for in enthusiasm. The people we prayed for, bless their hearts, actually seemed to like our unbridled delight in being able to pray for them.

At first, there didn't seem to be much happening, but we were so excited that we just kept on praying. We were encouraged by John Wimber's openness and honesty as we listened to his tapes. He said that he had prayed for people for nine months before God healed anyone. Then one day it finally happened for him. We thought, if *he* could pray for nine months without seeing anyone healed, then we can pray with no one getting healed just as well as he did! So we agreed to just keep trying. I have learned over the years the importance of tenacity. Possessing this attitude is imperative if you are going to break into the ministry of healing. If you want something, DO NOT GIVE UP! God loves a tenacious heart. He is a rewarder of those who diligently seek Him. Our antics back then seem laughable (maybe because they were), but, I'm telling you, hunger and tenacity are keys in moving out in this.

Actually, it wasn't long before we started seeing things happen. About that time John Wimber held a conference in Chicago. We went to hear him speak and watched closely to see how he went about ministering to people. The next Sunday we went back to our church incredibly enthused. The pastor happened to ask anyone who wanted healing to please stand up. One woman stood up, followed by several others. Here was our opportunity, in church of all places, and we were going to take full advantage of it! The three of us practically scrambled, like sheep let out of a pen, to get to them.

We each ended up with a different person. I got to the first woman who had stood up. Other church members joined us. When I asked what she needed prayer for, she said that she actually didn't need healing. She had been trying to pass her driver's license test and had failed it twice. She wanted prayer so that she could pass her third and final chance at the exam. All that anticipation and she didn't want healing! Disappointed, I wondered to myself, "I don't know if this will work for that!" Nevertheless, we prayed.

Part of learning to pray for the sick is learning to recognize God's presence on people. Certain visible signs or reactions often accompany God's working in a person. (I will discuss this in a more systematic way later.) People will sometimes tremble, feel certain things, do certain things. As we prayed, the signs of God's presence came on this woman in a strong way. And we were merely praying for her to pass a driver's license test! I was thrilled to see what was happening. She, too, was excited, because she was desperate—she had failed the test miserably before. Now realize, we were not asking God to supernaturally give her the answers to her test so that she could go out and be a threat to everyone on the road. She had been so nervous the first two times she had taken the test that she had forgotten everything she knew and had only gotten about fifty percent right. God must have done something that day—she came back the next week and reported that not only had she passed the test but she had also gotten a nearly perfect score! To her it was a miracle. I was impressed. Wow, I thought, this even works for driver's tests—now that's cool!

The Ministry of All Believers

During this time we saw God touch more and more people. A woman who had been given little hope to live was healed of a fast moving, aggressive cancer.

One of the most exciting developments for me was that the more things happened, the more *other* people got excited too. Doing the best we could, my friends and I taught them everything we knew. It wasn't a lot, but we could say, "God's here. Go for it!" They did and prayers for healing started spreading.

More and more people became involved in praying for the sick and for other needs as well. It was happening in homes, businesses, hospital rooms and on sidewalks. People were suddenly moving in the power of the Lord quite effectively. Some were very attuned to hearing God's voice, some empowered in leading worship, and others moved out in intercessory prayer, counseling, serving, evangelism and pastoring. In partnering with the Holy Spirit, believers were amazingly effective.

Then it hit me. This was the Second Reformation. It had snuck up and caught me unaware! The reality was far more than I had ever thought or imagined. Ministry was truly in the hands of the people. Many were suddenly responding to individual calls to minister in various ways and doing it very effectively. This was it, and I could see that the key was the Holy Spirit. Yes, maturity, wisdom and the attitudes of our heart are critical. That's what this book is about. But it is the Holy Spirit Himself who brings reformation. He is the Great Reformer.

> **This was the Second Reformation. It had snuck up and caught me unaware!**

A New Approach to Prayer

After I started moving in what was, for me, a new way of praying for people, I started to analyze what was different about this approach. I finally concluded that two things were radically different. Although others may have always prayed this way, these ways were new to me.

Asking for His Presence

First, I used to pray to God somewhere "out there" to do something "down here." Now I prayed, "God, we ask You to come." I asked for His presence. Describing his experience before he learned to effectively pray for healing, John Wimber once said, "We had often felt the presence of God in worship. We would feel His presence come; the air would even feel thick at times. But we never realized that His presence and His power were the same thing." That was the key. Where His presence is, His power is. Where His presence is, faith comes—as well as everything else that we need.

John 5:19

Second, instead of trying to figure out what I should have God do next, I began trying to understand what God, who was here, was doing so that I could go along with it. John 5:19 says, "Jesus did only what He saw the Father doing." If that's how Jesus operated, shouldn't we be doing the same thing? We can be sure God has a good idea what He wants to accomplish! It's always better to do what He wants than what we want. If we can grasp what He's doing and follow, a lot will happen.

My whole approach to praying had changed. Now, I asked God to come and, when He came, tried to flow along with what He was doing. Someone on our team might get an impression that the Lord wanted to touch a man across the room, so we would go over to him and pray, "God, come and minister to this man." Basically, God did the whole thing. We watched Him work

This approach takes the pressure off us. When someone comes for prayer, we don't have to be afraid, thinking "I don't know if I have that in me!" It really has nothing to do with you or me. It's all God. We can be at ease. We can say, "I don't know what God is going to do right now, but let's ask Him to come so we can find out." It can be a lot of fun, an adventure, because we never know what's next! He does something different every time. He is always creative; every time He works is wonderful and unique.

That's why, no matter how many times I minister in meetings, I always look forward to seeing what God will do next. For instance, in one meeting we were praying for Lena, a sweet ninety-three year old lady. After praying for a while we finally figured out that God wanted Lena to pray for *us*. As soon as she started to pray she began giving words to us that were obviously from the Lord. The healing presence of the Lord was in her hands. Afterwards, she shared that in her youth she had been a nurse. Her job, at times, had been to carry infants who had just died to the morgue. She recalled how her hands got colder and colder as she carried their lifeless bodies down the stairs. But this night, as she spoke and placed her hands on those who needed healing, she felt her hands get warmer and warmer—in fact, unusually hot! Not only was God healing us, but He was also healing one of her saddest memories. It was one of the most moving experiences of my life. Who could have known what was going to happen? Who can out-create the Creator?

God is teaching us all the time, often through each other. It's an adventure. We may not know where He will take us, but we do know that He is with us on the way. That's the best part of this journey, walking with God. And when we walk with God, anything can, and does, happen!

Tips for Getting Started

• **Read Scriptures on healing.** Read what Jesus did and how He did it. Let Him be your role model. As you read, put yourself in His shoes, then in the shoes of those being healed and imagine what it must have been like having the power and heart of God revealed.

• **Find someone** or some others who share your interest and desire in praying for others and get together with them.

• **Ask God** to launch and direct you into the fullness of the journey He has for you.

• **See more references** in the bibliography.

2
The Holy Spirit

While this book will introduce many tools for ministry, what is of primary importance is not a tool at all. It is the Holy Spirit. In truth, we are a tool to be used by Him. All ministry is His and He gives us the privilege of partnering with Him in it. Hopefully, as we see Him work, our delight will not be in our own ministry, but in Him, and all that He does will continually amaze us. It is only fitting to begin a book such as this with a discussion of the Holy Spirit: who He is, what happens when He comes, and what it is like when we partner with Him.

Acts One

When someone is about to leave us, their last words are often important. This certainly must have been true of Jesus, whose words were always well chosen and laden with importance. The last words Jesus spoke before He ascended into heaven are recorded in Acts.

> On one occasion, while He was eating with them, He gave them this command, "Do not leave Jerusalem, but wait for the gift my Father has promised, which you have heard me speak about. For John baptized with water, but in a few days you will be baptized with the Holy Spirit. ... You will receive power when the Holy Spirit comes on you; and you will be my witnesses in Jerusalem, and in all Judea and Samaria, and to the ends of the earth." After he said this, he was taken up before their very

eyes, and a cloud hid him from their sight. (Acts 1:4-5,7-8)

After years of being with Him, living with Him, seeing Him work and being trained for ministry by Him, Jesus told them not to do *anything* until something crucial happened—until after they received the coming Holy Spirit. Although the coming of the Holy Spirit begins in Acts 2, the rest of the book continues to describe the experience of which Jesus spoke.

The book of Acts begins: "In my former book [the book of Luke] I wrote about all that Jesus began to teach and do until the day He was taken up to heaven." The word *began* is significant—it implies that Acts is an account of what Jesus *continued* to do after He rose to heaven. Instead of one person, Jesus, doing all the things written about in the book of Luke—speaking His powerful words and doing His awesome works—suddenly Jesus begins to act via the Holy Spirit through *every* believer. This initiates what has to be one of the devil's worst nightmares: instead of one Jesus at work, there are now millions and millions of "Jesuses" walking around, doing what He did!

It's interesting to note that the book of Acts ends rather abruptly. I think it is a message to us that there is no ending to the book of Acts! The acts of the Holy Spirit continues, now through us.

> **When Jesus uses the word *baptism* to describe the outpouring, the connotation was a dousing — the Holy Spirit being poured out in great abundance.**

In Acts 1:5 Jesus used the word *baptism* to describe the outpouring of the Holy Spirit. This is an interesting choice of words. In the Old Testament, the pouring of the Holy Spirit upon people was often described by the word *anointing*, pouring a vial of oil over the person. But when Jesus uses the word *baptism* to describe the outpouring, the connotation was a dousing—the Holy Spirit being poured out in great abundance.

The word baptism can also denote an entrance into something new—you will never be the same again! But, we should add, this does not mean that the outpouring of the Holy Spirit in our lives is just a one-time experience. That is simply not enough! Acts 4 describes an event after Pentecost where the Spirit was poured out upon many of the same individuals who received Him in Acts 2. The baptism with the Holy Spirit is ongoing. You have entered into something new—a wave has crashed over you, but it never dries. Don't limit yourself; you can expect many outpourings of the Holy Spirit. This has been my experience repeatedly.

Who is the Holy Spirit?

It is helpful to describe, even if imperfectly, who the Holy Spirit is. He is God. He is a person, one of the persons of the Trinity. Each member of the Trinity has a personality and we are invited to know each personally and intimately. Briefly describing the members of the Trinity will help us understand the Holy Spirit.

First, God comes to us as our Father—the One who created us. He looks at us with love, saying, "I created you and I am very pleased with what I made in you." That's the Father, your Father. He is awesome, yet close to us. The words, "Our Father, who art in heaven," combine the picture of the staggeringly almighty God who fills the heavens with a picture of a Father filled with love and closeness to His child. The combination is mind-boggling. Looking out into space on a starry night, I can hardly comprehend that its Creator knows, loves and is a father to *me*. The Father.

God comes to us in the person of the Son—the One who wore flesh like ours and felt what we feel. He came and perfectly revealed to us what God is like. He took our sins upon Himself—the Lamb of God. He died in our place that we might live. He is everything to us; we want to be like Him and we want to be with Him. We are forever grateful for the price only He could have paid. He is our passion. The Son.

In the person of the Holy Spirit we encounter God closely and personally. In this life, this is how we usually experience God's presence. For that reason I will use the terms *the presence of God* and *the Holy Spirit* interchangeably. In both the New Testament Greek and the Old Testament Hebrew the word for Spirit also means breath or wind (in Greek, *pneuma*; in Hebrew, *ruach*). He is so intimate; we share the same breath. He is something that fills us—as close as the air inside us. Yet, at the same time, He is a wind that is beyond us; He can be gentle, yet He can also blow down everything in His path. God, awesome and close. The Holy Spirit.

Levels of God's Presence

Sometimes using the phrase *when the Holy Spirit comes* brings a very good question to people's minds: Isn't God everywhere all the time? How can I say, *when He comes*? When we look at the verses in Scripture that describe God being in a place, we find that there are various intensities, or levels, of God's presence.

1. God is Everywhere

The first level acknowledges that God is everywhere all the time. He is omnipresent. Psalm 139:6-10 says, "Such knowledge is too wonderful for me; it is high, I cannot attain to it. Where can I go from your Spirit? Where can I flee from Your presence? If I ascend into heaven, You are there. If I make my bed in hell, behold, You are there. If I take the wings of the morning, and dwell in the uttermost parts of the sea, even there Your hand will lead me." The Psalmist is saying that no matter where we go, God's presence is there. This is very comforting, because we may find ourselves in places where we really want Him with us! And He is. He is always there.

2. God Indwells Believers in a Special Way

John 14 describes another level of His presence, His indwelling presence. This second level is special for believers in Jesus. Jesus spoke of Himself, the Father and the Holy Spirit as dwelling with us and in us. In John 14:20 He said, "At that day you'll know that I am in the Father, and you in Me, and I in you." This is an amazing, mind-boggling reality: that Jesus—yes, God Himself—dwells within us! The more we learn about how awesome God truly is, the more staggering His dwelling within us becomes.

3. God Comes More Intensely at Times

There are some Scriptures that describe yet another level: when God's presence comes more intensely at times, usually for a particular purpose. One example is found in Luke 5:17. "Now it happened a certain day, as Jesus was teaching, that there were Pharisees and teachers of the law sitting by, who had come out of every town in Galilee and Jerusalem; and *the power of the Lord was present to heal them*" (emphasis mine). The phrase I put in italics is easy to overlook. It shows that the Father was doing something unusual here—an extraordinary level of His presence was there for a particular purpose, in this verse, to heal. Another example of this level of His presence is found in Psalm 22:3, where it says that God inhabits the praises of His people. Often during worship an awareness of the presence of the Lord suddenly sweeps over all. He is near in a way that is different from before. At such times I have seen even unbelievers weep, feeling something, a closeness to God, they have never felt before.

4. God's Overwhelming Presence

Some Scriptures describe a level of God's presence that is *overwhelming*—more than a human being can handle. When His presence comes with such intensity, a person is undone—physically, emotionally or both.

In his book, *When the Spirit Comes with Power*, John White writes about people, both in Scripture and recent history, experiencing God at various levels. At the level of His overwhelming presence, sometimes words cannot describe the emotional shock of experiencing God's reality and holiness. White describes an experience that he himself had as "both terrifying and full of glory" (pp. 87-88). This awe, often overlooked today, makes the reality of our access to the Father through Jesus' death amazing—and truly, without His enabling grace, it is an impossibility.

When Moses met the Lord on the mountain, the attitude of the people was, in essence, "If we go up the mountain where His presence dwells, we will be killed." (See Exodus 20:19.) They were not exaggerating or misinformed. Moses alone approached God because he was desperate to know Him. God loves that desperation! He responds to the determination that even if His presence were to kill us, we want Him so badly that we will go anyway. When Moses did get to see God's presence, God had to shield Moses from His fullness in the cleft of a rock so that he would not die (Exodus 33:20).

> **Moses alone approached God because he was desperate to know Him.**

Daniel 8:16-18 gives us an example of how a person can be physically overwhelmed by this level of God's presence.

> I heard a man's voice between the banks of the Ulai, who called and said, "Gabriel, make this man understand the vision." So he came near where I stood. And when He came, I was afraid, and fell on my face. But He said to me, "Understand, son of man, that the vision refers to the time of the end." Now as He was speaking to me, I was in a deep sleep with my face to the ground. But when He touched me, He stood me upright.

Even though the speaker was not actually God, but an angel, the presence of the Lord was so intense that Daniel fell to the ground like a dead man. Daniel couldn't move until the angel came and touched him. The aftermath of this incident is described in verse 27. "And I, Daniel, fainted and was sick for days; afterwards I arose, and went about the king's business; but I was astonished by the vision. No one understood it." He was so undone that even afterwards he fainted and was physically affected for days.

The Book of Revelation offers another example. Here the apostle John is talking—John who had known Jesus in the flesh for years. He was the disciple who was as close as a brother to Him, the one who put his head upon Jesus' breast at the Last Supper. But in Revelation 1:17, John says, "And when I saw Him, I fell at His feet as dead. And He laid His right hand on me, saying to me, 'Don't be afraid, I am the First and the Last.'" John had now encountered Jesus in His overwhelming glory.

There are more accounts of people being undone by the presence of the Lord. The Transfiguration (Matthew 17:6-7) and Paul's encounter with Jesus on the road to Damascus (Acts 9:1-9) describe such events. II Chronicles 7:2 speaks of the presence of the Lord filling the second temple to such an extent that the priests could no longer stand to minister.

There are times when we may encounter God at each of these levels. However, the boundary between them is not sharp. Sometimes we may experience a partially overwhelming presence of the Lord through which we can actually live and perhaps not even faint, but it may have effects on our frail (in comparison with God) humanity.

> **Sometimes we may experience a partially overwhelming presence of the Lord through which we can actually live and perhaps not even faint, but it may have effects on our frail humanity.**

What It's Like When the Holy Spirit Comes

What is it like when the Holy Spirit comes? In Acts 8 His presence was so obvious that Simon, an unbeliever, wanted to buy what he saw. I think that sometimes today we treat the subject of the Holy Spirit like the story of the Emperor's New Clothes. In this story it was said that only a fool could not see the clothes the emperor was supposedly wearing. The people could see the emperor was naked, but they were afraid to step out and admit that they did not actually see his clothes. Too often the Holy Spirit is waiting for us to ask for Him to come in a profound way, but no one wants to admit that He is not here in that way already, so no one seeks. In the life and times recorded in Acts 8, it wasn't like that at all. His presence and activity were clear. Although Simon's motive for wanting to buy the power for himself was altogether wrong, the incident shows us that the presence of the Holy Spirit must have been very, very obvious.

Of course, it is true that His presence might not be obvious to everyone at all times. Sometimes He comes in a quiet way. In 1 Kings 19, God wasn't in the earthquake. He wasn't in the fire or in the whirlwind; He was in the whisper. Sometimes His presence is so subtle, it's almost like the touch of a butterfly wing. At other times, His presence is very obvious. It is normative to experience both. Looking at our own lives and times, we need to ask ourselves, "Does our experience of the Holy Spirit match the fullness and reality described in Scripture, or are we playing 'Emperor'?"

When the Holy Spirit comes, people's experiences today are quite similar to those recorded in Scripture. First, they often experience the fruit of the Spirit. They may feel a profound sense of love or the freedom of His joy. Perhaps, for the first time in their lives, they experience a true peace. We sometimes don't realize how precious peace can be to a person whose life has been in constant turmoil—it could be the greatest thing in his or her entire life.

People also experience the Spirit's gifts. That was certainly the case in the book of Acts. There the gifts of prophecy and tongues are frequently mentioned as accompanying the outpouring of the Spirit. Years ago we prayed for a couple who had just come to the Lord after God caused a startling turnaround in the condition of the husband's father, who had been close to death. One night we prayed that they receive an outpouring, or baptism, of the Spirit. We could sense the Spirit's strong presence, although not too much happened visibly at the time. Later we found out that the next day the husband had gone into their barn and had a remarkable vision from the Lord. Afterwards both he and his wife experienced God's presence and such a hunger for His Word that they stayed home and read their Bibles the entire day. (That insatiable hunger for the Word went on for years; eventually they left everything to pursue Bible school.) Every so often their cousin, who was on our prayer team, would get a telephone call from them or from one of their other family members who had also come to the Lord in that season. One call was to say, "We were praying and sometimes it was like God was saying things through us!" Another call was to report, "We started praying in a foreign language! We don't know what we're saying!" Their cousin would tell them that was okay, it was normal, and tell them about the gifts of the Spirit. They had no notion what to expect; the Spirit was moving faster than we could teach them!

The overwhelming or partially overwhelming presence of God can also cause physical responses within us. It's like an overloading of our nervous system—God's presence can be more than we can handle! People may tremble and shake. Their eyelids may flutter, or they may feel sensations of warmth, heat or electricity. Sometimes they feel like they are in a gentle rain. It is interesting that in Scripture, the effects of the Holy Spirit are often compared to the wind (John 3:8, Acts 2:2), rain (Joel 2:23), or fire (I Thess. 5:19, Acts 2:3). People's emotions can be peaked; they may weep easily or can't help but laugh. These responses can be deeply healing for people. There is often a profound story behind the outward appearance. If you see something strange, you may want to talk to the person afterwards before judging it by the way it looks.

Let me interject that a specific experience or reaction is not a certain sign that the Spirit is present. The Spirit can do a profound and deep work with no outward evidence. Sometimes the signs may be experienced later. And it is also possible to see signs like those I've described when the Spirit is not behind them at all. If that is true, why even tell you about these signs?

Applications for Team Ministry

First, I mention them so that when you see them, you will not be shocked or alarmed. When you sense the Holy Spirit's presence and things begin to happen, you can reassure others that such things often happen and help them keep focused on the Lord. Second, signs can help you track what the Holy Spirit is doing. When I was a teacher, I found it very useful to recognize confusion on my students' faces. If I saw it, I could backpedal and re-explain a concept until I could see that it was understood. It improved my effectiveness as a teacher. In the same way, we are more effective as ministry team members if we are alert to the possible effects of the Holy Spirit. Sometimes we may pray and nothing seems to happen. Then someone speaks a word and suddenly we see signs of God's presence. That might be a clue to follow the direction of that word for a while! (It is also often beneficial to ask the person you are praying for what is going on; they might tell you something of which you are unaware.)

Years ago we were working with a group of college students doing this type of ministry. One day they called and said that the husband of one of their professors had a brain tumor. They had asked her if we could come over and pray, and she said yes. I felt a mixture of elation (remember how excited we were to find someone who needed prayer back then?) and terror, because she was a fellow professor and now this exciting facet of my life would be out of the bag! Our group met with the two of them in a small dormitory chapel and went for it! As we were praying, one of the students silently motioned to the rest of us, mouthing words that there was a sensation of an unusual amount of heat over one part of the man's head; she could actually feel it as she moved her hand over the spot. We all placed our hands near that spot, blessing what the Holy Spirit was doing and asking Him to do even more. A few days later one of the students talked to the professor and asked what she and her husband thought. Both of them had been surprised and deeply touched by the compassion of the students and the feeling in the room when we prayed. The professor said her husband asked her how everyone knew where to lay their hands. When she asked him how he knew they were in the right place, he told her that his doctor had tattooed a small ink dot over the spot so that he could find it again. It was hidden by his hair and was so little that no one but the doctor would even notice. However, it was a little sensitive, so he knew that they were touching exactly the right spot when they prayed. That was the Holy Spirit showing us what to do. As we desire to do "only what we see the Father is doing" (John 5:19), God develops a language with us, a way of communicating, so that we are able to follow Him in His ministry.

By the way, that man did get better. In his next x-ray, the tumor had shrunk dramatically. Other people were praying, too. I'm not suggesting that God healed him because of our prayer and not that of others. All prayers are important. (I will discuss in a later chapter how different prayers work together.) Clearly God had done a work!

Our Changed Lives

When we encounter the Spirit's presence, our lives are never the same again. As He lives in us, the Spirit imparts fruit and gifts and, although it may take a while to discover, He gives us direction deep within. Significant other changes happen as well. We are launched into a pursuit of God. Our love of worship is very often deepened. We are ruined for other things that had captured us before; they suddenly become pale in the face of the reality and wonder of God Himself. We are set on a pursuit of true holiness, closeness with Him, adoration of His character, and love for His works and ways. There is also a joyful willingness to embrace the cross: less of ourselves, more sacrifice for the sake of the kingdom, and the "brokenness" where God chooses to dwell (Isaiah 57:15).

Most important, in this encounter with the Holy Spirit, we enter a new phase of our life and come into a nearness to and friendship with Him. This is a time of getting to know Him, realizing how close He is, listening to His voice and learning of His ways as He illuminates the Word, telling us what He is doing in our lives and in the world around us.

And this—which is what this book is about—is how God brings us into a life of Spirit-led ministry. This relationship, this friendship with the Holy Spirit is an absolute key for ministry. When we are ministering to someone, we are constantly talking to our best friend and counselor, asking, "Holy Spirit, what is going on here? What is Your heart for this person? What pleases You about them? What are You doing with them tonight?" Or, "Why isn't anything happening right now? Oh, you mean that's what I should do! What should I say? How should I say it?" An underlying intimate interaction is going on as you partner with the Holy Spirit in ministry.

> **An underlying intimate interaction is going on as you partner with the Holy Spirit in ministry.**

Two Important Attitudes of our Heart

I have found that two heart attitudes are important in our life with the Holy Spirit: *love* and *desire*. Both of these are found in 1 Corinthians 14:1: "Follow the way of love and eagerly desire the spiritual gifts, especially the gift of prophecy." The word for *follow the way (dioko)* means pursue, seek after, strive for, run after. That's what we're supposed to do with love—love for God and love for people. The word for *eagerly desire (zeloo)* is one of the strongest words in the Bible, often translated as *covet*. It is something we must want badly. We are to strongly desire *spiritual gifts (pneumatikos)*. Literally in the Greek, the phrase is *the things of the Spirit*. We must desire *Him* and *all* He has.

There is something about desire that God loves. We are told, "You have not because you ask not . . . Seek and you shall find . . . God is a rewarder of those who diligently seek

Him" (James 4:2, Matthew 7:7, Hebrews 11:6). These verses are exhorting us to desire—with a tenacity to keep seeking until we find. Even though we already have God, we love Him with a desire that can almost feel like desperation at times. David, who already knew and had God, wrote, "As the deer panteth for the water, so my soul longs after You" (Psalm 42:1). Can't you see the deer standing in the woods panting? His tongue is hanging out, gasping for water! That's the degree of desire our feeling for the Lord should be. Like David, we are to want more.

Some people get upset when we talk about there being more—they do not want to hear that they do not have it all. I would simply ask them, are you still alive? Scripture says an encounter with the full extent of God's presence would kill us! Thus, the very fact that we are alive means that there must be more! God is infinite and we are finite. We will never be done knowing all of God. We will never be done seeking Him and all He has.

Are we desperate enough? Someone once said that it is a good idea for a church to ask itself, "If God didn't show up on a Sunday morning, would we know the difference?" It's a good question to ask ourselves individually, too. If God didn't show up in our lives for a period of time, would we notice? Would we see a difference? I can honestly say—because God has let me fall on my face so often—yes! I know the difference. I need Him desperately. It is a good thing to need Him. We can't do anything without Him. John Wimber used to say, "You don't want to see *my* ministry. Without God, it's awful. You want to see *His* ministry." Keep that desperation for His presence.

The Attitude of God's Heart

A while back, my family and I were reading a verse about God judging leaders more harshly than others. It caught my attention. Since I was a pastor, I thought it might be a good idea for me to understand what He meant! When I was praying about it, three very clear impressions came to me—three ways the Lord would judge leaders more harshly. I was surprised because I had never really thought about it before. First, I felt God saying He will judge leaders who have had people sit in their churches for years who have never been led into a true saving relationship with God. Second, I heard the warning in Jeremiah 8:11 about the priests healing the wounds of the people only superficially. We must heal them deeply. Third, I saw that God has given very precious gifts and callings to His people, and He will judge leaders who set aside these people, like jars on the shelves of the church, wasting their gifts and callings. Very sobering thoughts! But God can change all that.

In thinking about these three points, I found it interesting that they dovetail with what I have found to be the three most common themes on the heart of the Holy Spirit during a ministry session. Usually, when people come up for prayer ministry, God wants to either bring them closer to Himself (or to salvation), heal them deeply, or empower them (filling them, equipping them and/or speaking to their dreams and visions).

> **Usually, when people come up for prayer ministry, God wants to either bring them closer to Himself, heal them deeply, or empower them.**

The Holy Spirit has a heart for people. We need to have that heart. The movie and life of Patch Adams, about a man's non-traditional quest to become a doctor, resonated with me because, in many ways, it paralleled what I know about the heart of the Spirit. Patch had a heart for people; he was not into titles or positions. In the clinic he started, once he helped people heal, he used them to help bring healing to others. If the opportunity to help others was not there, he tenaciously found or made the opportunity. He was driven by a love for people. So should it be with us. God's heart is brimming with love for people, that they might come to Him, be healed by Him, and be launched into the adventure of their lives with Him. As we minister, may His heart beat in ours.

Tips for Walking with the Spirit

• **Read Jesus' promises to send the Holy Spirit.** In Luke 11:9-13, He says three times how we are to seek, three times how we will receive, three times how we will receive a good thing, and then how certain it is "our heavenly Father give the Holy Spirit to those who ask Him!"

• **Read how He came in the Book of Acts.** See, for example, Acts 2:1-47, 4:23-31, 10:44-48 and 19:1-7.

• **Ask for Him to come.** When alone, ask Jesus to come and pray for you the way you might have a prayer team member pray for you.

• **Talk to the Holy Spirit like you would a friend.** When praying for others, talk to Him about what you are seeing. Go for walks alone with Him and discuss what is going on in your life. Ask Him what is on His heart.

Bonding with God

It is a mistake to make the gifts of the Spirit, the ministry of healing, or any other *thing* our focus and goal. Our focus must always, first and foremost, be the Lord Himself. Seeking

Him first, however, in no way means we should neglect to seek the gifts and works of God. God tells us to *earnestly* desire them. If we use them with the right heart, as He intended, they can actually bond us more closely to God. John Paul Jackson, whose prophetic ministry has always reflected to me the heart of God, includes some incredible gems in his teachings about the prophetic gifts and the love of God. One of my favorites is about his relationship with his son. John Paul had been on the road ministering in different churches and wanted to give his young son more attention. Finally he had a weekend off and thought it would be a good idea to build his son the tree house he had always wanted. Driving to the lumberyard, he loaded up his truck with 32 two-by-fours. When he got home, he started lifting them out, about four at a time, to take them to the back yard where he was going to build the tree house. Walking by, he noticed his son looking at him with a deep expression of longing in his eyes. The thought came to John Paul, "Why are you doing this?"

"Well," he replied, "because my son wants a tree house."

"But what does he really want?"

Then it hit him. "It's to spend time with me."

So he asked his son if he'd like to help carry the boards. His son's face lit up. So one by one, John Paul would lift one end of a two-by-four, his son would lift the other, and slowly they would carry it to the backyard—32 times. What would have taken him about ten minutes took about an hour.

"But, you know," he reflected, "because of doing it together, both my son and I realized that something happened that day, a bonding like never before." He added, "Later, the Lord started speaking to me about this experience. 'John Paul, don't you think I could do the things you do without you? I could easily heal the sick, call people by name and speak truth into their lives. Why do you think I choose to do it with you? I do it because a bonding happens between us, like what happened between you and your son. We get to do it together.'" (*used by permission*)

Those words are so true. When we work together with God, we grow together. Our love for each other deepens. We are bonded. God loves us and wants His child to help his Dad in His work. I know from experience that when you see Him work, you're just not the same again. You are "ruined" because nothing else will do! You come to appreciate Him, His love, His gospel like never before when you so intimately see God at work, touching hearts and renewing lives. This becomes what you want to do with your life. You want to sell all you have and buy the field with this treasure in it.

> **You come to appreciate Him, His love, His gospel like never before when you so intimately see God at work.**

There is always more. And God will take our hands and let us partner with Him as we find it. As always, among all the treasures, He is the greatest treasure of all. As we find Him, we are left both deeply satisfied and hungrier to know Him more.

3

An Approach to the Ministry of Healing

God's desire to heal is evident throughout the Bible. In the Old Testament God often healed. One of His names was Yahweh Rapha, the God who heals (Exodus 15:26). In the New Testament, Jesus constantly demonstrated God's desire to heal. Jesus not only healed people, but He also taught His disciples how to heal and then sent them out with the command to heal (Matt. 10:1,8, Luke 9:2,10:9). Jesus healed people for several reasons. Foremost, it was His compassionate heart to do so. ". . . [He] saw a great multitude and was moved with compassion toward them and he healed their sick" (Matt. 14:14). Healing also demonstrated His reality and power to save. "'But that you may know that the Son of Man has authority on earth to forgive sins,' He said to the paralyzed man, 'I tell you, get up, take your mat and go home.'" (Luke 5:24). It was also a sign that God's Kingdom, in all its goodness, freedom and life, had come. It went hand in hand with Jesus' proclamation, "The Kingdom of God is here" (Mark 1:15). Can we say that any of these reasons for healing has changed, excusing us from praying for healing today?

If God wants to use us to heal people today, let's do it well. In this chapter I dive right into what ministry teams actually do when they pray for healing. When leading training sessions, I present this material early so that we can start practicing early. A significant part of the learning process comes by trying out what we talk about. Although healing is only one of the many things that ministry teams pray for, it is an excellent way to begin to learn how to pray—the goals of the prayers are clear and it helps develop a heart for people. It is also usually impossible to create a man-made solution; unless God shows up, nothing is going to happen!

The Five Step Prayer Model

As I mentioned in the first chapter, our approach to prayer is based upon asking for God's presence and then following the ministry that He desires to do. We do not follow our will—what we think is best—but we try to discern what God is already doing and follow Him. This is the way Jesus ministered: "I only do what I see the Father doing." (John 5:19).

> **Our approach to prayer is asking for God's presence and then following the ministry that He desires to do.**

John Wimber taught what he called the "Five Step" model for prayer. I like to call it the "Five Step Non-Model" because it actually steers you away from any preconceived notions about what should happen. Because every person and every situation is different, what God wants to do each time is different. The Five Step model teaches you to listen to the person and to listen to God so that you, like Jesus, can "do what the Father is doing."

Sometimes, the Holy Spirit may skip the first two steps of the prayer model and instantly tell you how to pray. If so, you don't need to follow the steps; follow Him! At other times you may start praying (step four) and then back up to get more information (step one). You don't need to be rigid about following this model, but I think you will find it useful as a guide.

1. The Interview

The first step is simply asking "How are you?" or "What do you want prayer for?" You want to find out the need—where it hurts. As you listen very carefully to the person's answer, you are simultaneously listening just as carefully to the Lord. You are gathering information in the natural, but also in the supernatural—from God. Sometimes, as the person is talking, you feel the Lord highlight a part of what he or she says; it seems to jump out at you. At times you might get an impression to ask a certain question. For instance, the woman you are praying for might be talking about a pain in her shoulder. You get an impression that you need to ask about her relationship with her husband. She confirms that it is the source of a lot of stress. The Lord has led you to the underlying cause (step two).

2. The Underlying Cause

This step is discerning what may be behind the condition the person is telling you about. Sometimes, there is nothing. People are sick because they are sick. (Don't prod for a cause if the Lord is not prompting you, or don't lay a "heavy" on the person implying he or she is sick because of some failure in his or her life. (John 9:1-3)) At other times, like the woman mentioned above, God might want to deal first with something besides the obvious.

What you want to know is where to begin. A person's problems are often like the layers of an onion. The Lord knows which layer to peel off first. The obvious problem may actually be in the third layer, but you won't get to that effectively unless God peels off the first two. So you ask the

Lord, "What are You doing here? What do You want to do first?" He might want to do one thing tonight, something else next week and something else after that. All you need to know is what God wants to do right now. That is what you actually pray for. I've often seen physical conditions, the need mentioned in step one, healed by dealing with underlying conditions.

3. Prayer Selection

Knowing what God wants to do leads into the third step. How does God want us to pray? What type of prayer should we use? Remember that the Spirit often wants to do one of three things—bring the person closer to God, heal the person, or bring equipping, empowerment, encouragement and/or vision. Many different categories of healing may be involved: physical healing, healing of emotions and past hurts, healing of the spirit (something that affects a person's relationship with God), healing of relationships, healing complicated by demonization, etc. The third step is choosing the first "arrow" to pull out of your quiver: what prayer is needed in this situation? Physical healing needs one approach; emotional healing may need another.

There are several different types of prayer that you can pray. *Petition* asks God to do or give something. The petition "Come, Holy Spirit" is always a good place to start, because we always need His presence. Later on, it might be, "Help, God, I don't have a clue what is going on! If You don't show up, I'm going to be in trouble!" *Intercession* (which I will cover in Chapter Seven) brings the person and his needs to God—and God and His presence to the person. *Prophetic* prayer, (also covered in Chapter Seven) is giving voice to God's words as He prays through us. Jesus used this type of prayer often. When He was praying for the blind man, He prayed a very short prophetic prayer: "See!" We can do that, too, but it can't be our own idea and not God's, or else nothing will happen! However, If it is God's idea and we say what He wants us to say, things can get interesting!

As you hold different tools in your hand, different arrows in your quiver, God may prompt you and let you know which one to use. Sometimes you're so lost, you don't know what to say, so you just start taking arrows out of your quiver and shooting them. Finally, one hits the mark. Then you feel God's presence come and you think, "So that's what God is doing! Okay, we'll go this route." Once you find the track God is laying, stick with it. Often, however, instead of "experimental praying" to find out what God is doing, it is best to not say anything but to wait for Him to speak to you or for His presence to come. Learn to be comfortable with silence. Filling this silence with words can sometimes detract from what God is doing.

4. Prayer Engagement

In the fourth step, we actually start praying. As we pray, we are asking, "What is the Father doing?" Contrary to what you might think, it does not hurt, nor does it interrupt prayer, to ask the person or the other prayer team members, "How are you doing? What are you feeling? Is anything happening?" It can often be very useful.

During prayer, you are trying to flow with what God is doing. You are like a midwife, helping to birth what God desires to do. If you don't see evidence of anything taking place, you can ask God, "What is going on here? Why isn't too much happening?" Perhaps He will answer, "This person feels unworthy. You need to address that first." The Lord will give you clues so that you can minister in the order He knows is best.

Because we depend on the Holy Spirit's presence and on knowing what He is doing, it is very useful to be able to see the effects of the Holy Spirit on the person. It is similarly useful to be able to discern God's voice and will (the subject of Chapter Eight). As prayer continues, sometimes you should change course, sometimes not. There is a "flow" to this type of ministry. When you are in the flow, you have to stay with it. When you do make a direction change, be sure it is the Lord's timing. Learning how to do this is sometimes better "caught" than taught. You will learn as you go along.

5. Post-Prayer Directions

The fifth step is what you do and say when the prayer is over. You might want to give some parting counsel. Be careful, however, not to turn prayer ministry into a counseling session—counseling is good, but it's for a different time and place. Too many words during prayer engagement can interfere with the flow of what God is doing. You may want to offer a referral, encourage getting involved in a small group, suggest reading something specific in the Word, or recommend a book. Be open to what the Spirit is saying at this stage, too. Mainly you want to express love and concern. Make it clear that you want to follow through; ask them to check back with you next week and let you know how they are doing. If something didn't happen during this session, tell them, "Let's pray again next week. We'll keep seeking God. Who knows what can happen!"

Suggestions on Praying for Healing

This prayer model avoids a "cookbook" approach to healing. God is always creative in what He does. An "if you see this, then do this" approach can keep you from asking God what He wants to do. I am constantly fascinated by the creative ways He ministers to every individual for whom we pray. Besides, God alone knows all the circumstances surrounding a situation. What may seem like a situation that automatically calls for a certain method may not actually be that kind of situation at all. We are better off constantly depending on Him to tell us what to do. Having said that, however, there is good advice and wisdom available regarding each of the broad categories of healing. There is obviously far more to learn than I am presenting here; we can profit much from our own experience and from what others have learned. I encourage you, however, to never think that you have completely understood how to pray for healing or that you have a methodology for every situation. Then we lose our dependence on Him.

Physical Healing

• Praying for physical healing may require patience waiting for His presence to come. Unless He does come, there is not much you can do, and it is often a test to see whether you will proceed without Him! With physical healing, I am more attuned to the visible signs that He is doing something than I am with other types of prayer ministry. (See Luke 8:46.) Therefore, in praying for physical healing, I usually pray with my eyes open. When giving a prophetic word or trying to listen to God, on the other hand, I sometimes close my eyes or look the other way so as not to be distracted by the person's expression.

• When healing does come, it really comes and the person usually knows it. Never pretend or let them pretend that they are healed when they are not. Don't be against doctors. They are blessings from God and on the side of healing. If the person wishes, encourage them to have their doctor check out how far their healing has progressed; I've found that this does not interfere with faith or God's supernatural activities. They may need to realize, however, that God's healing may be progressive. If God was doing something during the ministry session, His work may not be complete yet. We're dealing with reality here—God's works are real and testable!

Healing of the Spirit

• Healing of the spirit means resolving issues that affect a person's relationship with God. First we need to discern the problem. I have found it helpful to ask, "If you were to picture God standing in front of you, is anything keeping you from walking into His arms?" This question can uncover barriers such as guilt, shame, unconfessed sin, unforgiveness or an inaccurate picture of God (coming from an abusive father, for instance). If the issue is sin, help them confess it and repent. Then pronounce forgiveness. They may need to forgive themselves. If they were sinned against, they may need to forgive others. If the issue is one of inaccuracies about God, let the truth of Scripture shine, illuminating what God is really like and has done on their behalf. The Holy Spirit may show you unique ways to bring truth past people's barriers and into the recesses of their hearts, where the Word can effect a true and powerful change.

Healing of Emotions and Past Hurts

• In a prayer team setting, we must always remember that we are not counselors. We are there to bring the presence of God into lives. In doing this, your ministry will dovetail with any help they are receiving from trained counselors.

• In the prayer process, the Lord may prophetically bring into your mind or theirs an experience from their present or past for healing. Sometimes you may want to talk through this experience with the presence of Jesus shedding His marvelous light upon it, removing guilt and shame and perhaps breaking the power of words or continuing influences.

• Do not dig where the Spirit is not going and do not ever try to bring all of a person's issues to the surface at once. This can be overwhelming, hurtful and hopeless to the person. Only the Holy Spirit knows what to bring up and when. Often, after God heals something and covers it in His blood, He, as Corrie Ten Boon once said, places a "No Fishing" sign over it. Don't go fishing there—or do anything else that God is not doing!

Healing of the Demonized

• Demonization (this translation is much closer to the Greek than "demon possession") can come in various degrees—harassment, oppression and control. The more intense forms usually come into a person's life through gross sin, through being sinned against (often by physical or sexual abuse), or through the occult (including mind-altering drugs). Just because a person may have experienced these things does not mean he or she is necessarily demonized, but if you suspect demonization, check into these places of entry. A person does not suddenly become demonized just by walking down the street. Possible signs of demonization include obsessive behavior, uncontrollable thoughts, personality changes, an inability to worship God, and perhaps supernatural manifestations. Some physical and emotional problems not involving demonization may also have some of these signs, however, so don't jump to conclusions. Also, there may be other demon-induced maladies, like Peter's mother in-law's fever (Matt. 8:14, 15), that have none of these signs. Sometimes only God knows for sure.

• If sin is at the root, ask them to renounce it and repent. You cannot force a person to be free—you can only help them if they want freedom in the first place.

• Demons often act as "amplifiers" enhancing a person's problems and making them overwhelming. It is often best to deal with the person's sins or wounds first—these are often the demonic footholds. After dealing with the footholds, the person becomes "slippery" to demonic influence and the demons can easily be expulsed and prevented from coming back. Therefore, dealing with demonization proceeds like the other areas of healing as we deal with the footholds. Concentrate on bringing healing to the issues that the Lord puts in front of you and, if you get demonic interference with what you are doing, use your authority to stop it from interfering with the healing procedure.

• As with any type of healing, healing these issues may be somewhat instantaneous or a process. The speed may depend on the level of God's presence (I always ask for more!), but it can also depend on what God wants to do. As an analogy, I have known some people who were freed from alcoholism in an instant. Others went through a long process, but on the way God did profound things in many areas of their lives. Be ready to flow with whatever God is doing.

• When dealing with demons, watch out—they will want to choose the time, the place, and the way to fight, and they will try to hook your emotions to do it. They would love to take center stage, bring humiliation to the person, choose a time when you are exhausted, or make the person think they are bigger than they really are. Don't let them do any of this. You have authority to stop their interference with the ministry of Jesus in the person's life and can proceed to eliminate their footholds and thus their lifelines to the person. Sometimes, if knowing that demons might be involved would frighten the person, thus taking their eyes off Jesus and weakening their faith, it is best not to tell them demons are involved. You can command them under your breath and proceed with Jesus' powerful and glorious ministry. Leave the person filled with God, loving Him, and with a sword in their hand to stand their ground—eventually to be used to help others become free!

4

Values Underlying Our Approach to Team Ministry

The Lord can give us power in a day, and that is important—I don't intend to diminish its necessity—but it takes years to shape our character. Our character is precious to Him. In team prayer, or any kind of ministry, the Lord seems to spend more time on developing our character than anything else.

Within the Church, some groups have focused a lot on God's power and too little on His character, while others have focused more on His character but ignored His power. God is looking for those who combine both His character and His power. When that happens, the combination is explosive in its effectiveness for the kingdom.

When you operate in power, you reveal the power of an Almighty God, but your character helps reveal the heart of the Father, the compassion of Jesus, the closeness of the Spirit. This can do more than heal—it can change the course of someone's life.

Emphasis upon character is just one of the values that underlie our approach to ministry. A while ago I wished to communicate how we prayed for others so that newcomers could more easily understand and participate in our church's prayer teams. In writing down the values that underlie and shape what we do in team prayer ministry, I arrived at seven tenets upon which our ministry is centered.

1. Father-Centered

We want to care for each person like God the Father, with His love and compassion—to reveal the heart of a father toward his child. We want each one to know that He is *here* and that He *cares.*

2. Jesus-Centered

We want to focus on Jesus—His presence, His person, His character, His acts on our behalf. We know that if our focus is elsewhere—on demons, on ourselves or on anything else— like Peter, we will sink into the sea. But if Jesus is our passion—if our longing is to have Him with us, to have Him shine, to do what He would do in the way He would do it, and to communicate all He has done on behalf of the world—we are properly focused, able to rise upon the sea of whatever circumstances may face us.

3. Spirit-Centered

We desire to be led by the Spirit as completely as possible. We often need to be quiet to hear Him speak. People who are beginning to learn how to be led by the Spirit in prayer can feel very uncomfortable with waiting. I certainly felt this way when I started out. It can easily be several minutes before someone senses what the Lord is saying. There is a temptation to "keep the ball rolling" by leaping into the silence and saying something, but it is often far better to wait for the voice of the Lord. We must value this. At times we must make a conscious choice to be still and wait. A newcomer who is uncomfortable with silence might feel that those praying don't know what they are doing and jump in to do what they've done before in other church settings. They need to understand what is happening and respect what we are trying to do.

Sometimes, I shut my eyes and tune everything out and pray, "God, I just want to hear from You." Our prayer teams have learned to listen quietly for His voice, being sensitive to His promptings, His prophetic words and His giftings. We desire to move in His presence, power, anointing and heart.

4. Word-Centered

Everything we do must be Scriptural. We hold the power and counsel of the Word in high esteem.

By Scriptural I do not mean that every word we say must literally be found in the Bible. That would negate praying for a person to be a more anointed keyboard player, for instance. (Look up "keyboard" in your concordance!) In being Scriptural, I mean that we are in agreement with and do not do anything contrary to the advice, words, examples and spirit of the Bible, nor do we add anything new to our body of doctrine, which comes from Scripture alone. Although the Word is unchanging, I have found that God, through personal ministry, brings its message to people in ways which are wonderfully creative, amazingly powerful, and tailor-made to fit where they are in life. This never ceases to amaze me and always gives me greater appreciation of the wonder of His ageless Gospel.

5. Person-Centered

We focus on the person receiving ministry. (I usually begin a session by silently asking God what He sees as special about this person.) We must always listen carefully to that person, allowing them the opportunity to speak their heart. It is critical that we hold in absolute confidence what they share with us. (The only exception, as in counseling, is if their life or someone else's life is in danger. Then we would let the pastor know.) We are always sensitive to them and respect their dignity. Our heart is to help each person find God, find healing, and fulfill the call and purpose God has given to each person's life.

6. Learning-Centered

We want to be teachable. We don't want to "take over" ministry times, but allow the Holy Spirit to use everyone on the team and let everyone grow in ministry. Although God sometimes heavily anoints one person in a specific situation, He will use each one of us at various times and wants to raise us *all* up in ministry. If a person ignores this and, without the permission of the group leader, takes over a ministry session (especially a newcomer who does not know what we are doing and wants to "show everyone how to do it"), we consider this to be out of godly order.

When I first started leading our church's ministry teams, newcomers would occasionally jump in inappropriately, sometimes taking over ministry times. I wrote a handout on values, in part, to hand to people to diminish that likelihood. If reading it did not do the trick, I would have a more pointed talk with them to protect what we knew was precious in our ministry time.

You may wonder why we would allow a newcomer to participate at all. It is because we value learning. Our heart is not to be elite, but to constantly give away the ministry God has so graciously given to us. At the same time, we wish to give the best to those seeking prayer—if the ministry situation is a sensitive one, then, to protect the privacy of the one receiving prayer, we would not allow newcomers to participate. If it is not sensitive, as in praying for most physical healings, we want people to learn. Allowing even minimal participation can awaken a radical hunger for more. Even one-time visitors can take their hunger back to their home settings and seek God for more.

Each church or group must develop its own policy for newcomer participation. There are many options; your choice may depend upon the ministry setting. One option is to invite newcomers to watch and participate by talking to a team member who can then, if appropriate, relay the input to the person being prayed for. There also may be significant non-verbal ways in which they can participate. As you get to know people and feel that their levels of training, sensitivity and character are increasing, you can encourage them to do more and more.

> **As in an orchestra, each member needs humility and boldness — humility when it is someone else's turn to shine, boldness when the dancing hand of God rests upon us.**

Our desire is to follow the Spirit's lead and to be open to whatever He wants to do and to whomever He wants to use. 1 Corinthians 14 talks about the "manifest presence of God," which can be translated "the dancing hand of God." His hand can dance from person to person, and you never know where it will dance next! It is so much better to follow His hand than to follow our own ideas and desires. His hand may be with you one moment and move to someone else the next. We must be sensitive to allow each person to minister as they sense the Lord's prompting. Let the Lord use everyone, and let everyone grow in ministry. (Viva the Reformation!) A ministry team is like an orchestra and the "dancing hand of God" the orchestra leader. As in an orchestra, each member needs humility and boldness—humility when it is someone else's turn to shine, boldness when the dancing hand of God rests upon us.

7. Integrity-Centered

Integrity, openness and honesty are of utmost importance. When speaking prophetically, we must be honest in what we say God is speaking to us and how certain we are that He is saying it. If we are not certain, we can just say so. "I *think* God might be saying this. I'm not totally sure; see if it makes any sense." I've never found that this interferes with the power of a word that is given. If God is truly saying it, His Spirit floods in on the words. If it is God's word, it will not return void. We don't need to pump up the words with any authority of our own. Ministry with honesty and humility is *much* more effective than bravado.

In reporting healings, we must always be honest and must not exaggerate. There will be times when the healings we pray for don't take place. We must be open about it, be careful not to place a burden of failure on the person prayed for, and always offer to pray again at another time.

Your openness and honesty not only demonstrate your team's integrity to those for whom you pray, but also show them that your faith is based upon reality, not hype. This will impart the same sort of faith to them and will be rich in producing results. Don't try to shortcut values such as these. Without them you can slide down a slippery slope fast and the long-term effectiveness of your ministry can easily end up on the trash heap. If you slip in a value, apologize and quickly get back to operating in the character of Jesus. He will help you walk in His character if that is your heart.

Basically, this chapter can be summed up in John the Baptist's words: "He must increase, but I must decrease" (John 3:30). That is, we must nail our "flesh" to the cross, live in Him, and allow Him and all His character to be seen in what we do. We want to be natural yet supernatural, sensitive yet courageous, not pretending to be more than we are, yet exuding Jesus. He can make all this happen.

Tips to Encourage Godly Values In Your Teams

• **Encourage prayer team members to participate in small groups,** to be accountable to each other, to be transparent, and to pray for each other, dealing with whatever issues are in their lives.

• **Stress having godly character.** (I will talk more about its importance throughout the book.) Talking about how you prioritize it in your own life will encourage others to prioritize it in theirs.

• **Reproduce the review of the values** discussed in this chapter found in Appendix A for distribution to your prayer teams or to visitors who don't know what is going on.

• **Use the sample guidelines for team ministry** found in Appendix B as a basis for developing your own set of guidelines for your teams.

5
Faith

Throughout the Gospels Jesus constantly talks about faith: "Great is your faith," "Your faith has made you whole," "Your faith has saved you." Faith is important for everything. It is essential for salvation—salvation comes by grace, but through faith. Faith is what receives it. It is also important in healing. Jesus did very few miracles in His hometown "because of their lack of faith" (Mark 6). Faith is the God-given capacity to receive almost everything from Him.

It is possible to have faith and, therefore, receive things from God, even the miraculous, yet not walk in holiness or be pleasing to God (1 Cor. 13:2, Matt. 7:22-23). The miraculous does not validate a person or a ministry. On the other hand, faith is a vital element to walking the walk of God. Romans 14:23 and Hebrews 11:6 go so far as to state that unbelief, not having faith, is sin.

In team ministry faith is essential. Without it, we cannot receive anything. Although faith may be hidden, there must be faith somewhere. If it is not in the person you are praying for, then it must be in those who are praying. Sometimes God will just show up and give it to someone.

Because faith is so vital, it is very important to understand what faith is and how to use it. Often, however, it is so misunderstood that people either give up trying to grow in it or think they have already arrived.

The Challenge of Faith

When I first became a Christian, I began to read the Bible incessantly, as if for the first time. Jesus' words about faith fascinated me. I was determined to know more about it. My naïve applications of the verses about faith often bordered on the absurd and even the ridiculous, but I usually do things whole-heartedly. I remember one time, after reading that faith can move mountains, I stared at a piece of paper trying to drum up enough faith to make it move. (I figured I had to start somewhere!) Another time I became convinced that if I had enough faith I would never have another cold. I eagerly told my colleagues at work about it. About three weeks later I had a cold that was so bad there was no hiding it! My nose was dripping, my eyes were watering and spittle dribbled down my chin every time I coughed. The only thing good about it was I felt too awful to care what my friends thought about my newfound freedom from the cold virus.

Even if you don't follow the route of my unusual early approach to faith, you may still convince yourself that you understand faith until one day you read a verse like Mark 11:22-24:

> "For whosoever says to this mountain, 'Be moved, be cast into the sea,' and does not doubt in his heart but believes that these things will be done, will have whatever he says. So I say to you, whatever you ask for when you pray, believe that you will receive them, and you will have them."

If that is not challenging enough, it says in the book of John that we will do even greater works than Jesus and that *whatever* we ask, he will do (John 14:12-14). How do you deal with verses like these? Unless you've been moving mountains lately or walking on water, it is a challenge to explain what these texts are saying. Some people try to fit these Scriptures into their experience (or lack of it) and theologize their meaning away—or, at least, dilute it. But that's not being honest with these texts. The only thing to do is leave them as a challenge: the challenge of faith. These promises are out there, and as much as I wish I could attain every verse in the Bible, I will not lower the bar just so I can pretend to reach them. I will leave the bar where Jesus put it and go after it. I don't know how I'm going to get there, but I want to grow and learn and do more and more. To me, this is the only honest way to look at such verses. In the very pursuit of trying to attain to this height, we start learning more about faith—what it is, what it isn't, and how to move in it.

Faith 101: Believing *That* vs. Believing *In*

What is faith? Let me start from the beginning and lay a foundation to build on. Before I do that, however, let me clarify some terminology. In the Greek, the noun *faith* and the verb *believe* have the same root; they are essentially two forms of the same word. Therefore, whether I use the words *faith* or *belief* or *believing*, I am talking about the same thing.

The first important distinction to make is between believing *that* and believing *in*. James 2:19 says, "You believe that there is one God . . . Even the demons believe that—and shudder." What we are after, then, is not just a matter of believing *that*—believing a fact. Believing *that* is a requirement, but not nearly enough. We want to believe *in*.

There is a famous illustration of a man walking over Niagara Falls on a tightrope pushing a wheelbarrow. He goes across, comes back, and then asks everyone watching, "Who believes that I can do it again?" Just about everyone raises their hand. If he did it once, he can probably do it again. So he asks, "Very well, then, who will get in the wheelbarrow?" That is the difference between believing *that* and believing *in*. If you believe *in* you will get in the wheelbarrow and go for the ride. That is what God is calling us to do. It makes a big difference in our Christian walk.

Biblical faith is about a relationship, not about a state of mind. It is a relationship of love and trust in God. We are in the wheelbarrow and the Lord is taking us for the ride of our lives. Sometimes we are high above Niagara Falls, gripping the sides of the wheelbarrow, screaming. Other times we are exhilarated and can look out and say, "Wow, look at this view!" Our walk with God is an adventure. That's the kind of relationship we are talking about—a relationship of faith.

Believing *In* and Pruning

What we put our faith *in* must always be God. That sounds simple, but it is easy to get off track. We believe *in* God; we don't believe *in* faith. It's not having faith in faith. We don't have faith in our own state of mind, faith in formulas (if I do this, then God will do that), faith in circumstances, or faith in anything but Him. (We do have faith in His Word, assuming we interpret it correctly, but that really is believing in God.) If we put our faith anywhere but in God Himself, God may "pull the plug" on whatever we are trusting in. Early in our spiritual life He may let us walk on a foundation that is weak or not quite correct to let us experience how wonderful faith is. Eventually, He will decide it is time to strengthen and correct our foundation. Then it's time for pruning.

> **What we put our faith *in* must always be God. That sounds simple, but it is easy to get off track.**

John 15 is Jesus' major teaching on pruning. Several dominant themes run throughout the chapters before and after. One of these themes is faith. The context of John 15, therefore, indicates that a primary purpose of pruning is to produce greater faith. Peter's impending denial of Jesus, also threaded throughout these chapters, can be viewed as an illustration of pruning—for the purpose of establishing Peter's faith on more solid ground. While our circumstances may not be as dramatic as Peter's, we, too, may be pruned. If you have believed in something and suddenly everything you are standing on seems to fall through and you think, "What's happening here? Can I ever believe in anything again? Will my faith ever be the same?" God may be using your circumstances to prune you and give you greater faith.

If you were to graph your faith, it might start out at a seemingly high level and suddenly dive into a valley. When you are down, however, you often don't even know that you are in a valley—or if there will be an upward slope to the curve again! But God has a purpose in mind: to ground your faith in Him, not in anything else. If we depend on anything else but God and it is removed or broken, it's like suddenly walking without the crutch we had become accustomed to depending upon. It may be awful and awkward for a long time! Sometimes you think your faith will never be strong again.

However, the truth is that once your faith is grounded on Him alone, it will be stronger than ever. There *is* an up-slope that you are heading towards. You will end up much higher than you were when you began and, from there, you can move into the higher levels of faith He has promised.

I have been in that valley. I started high, but what I thought was faith was really a trust in my own understanding and formulas. When God finally began pulling the plug so that my faith could be based on a true foundation, I went through a valley that lasted several years. I didn't think I would ever come out. I didn't know that I could simply trust that God is here and that He is good. I thought I had to understand and predict everything He was going to do. Actually, it was a question of who was in control. Who was pushing the wheelbarrow? I had to learn that sometimes I need to get into the wheelbarrow without knowing where He is going. But we will all experience far more incredible adventures and see many more awesome works when He is doing the steering.

Often people who have been pruned walk "with a limp" like Jacob yet move in incredible faith, humility and works. Scripture is full of examples. Peter is one. He began high on the faith curve, thinking his faith and love for Jesus would never fail, even thinking he would give his life for Him (John 13:37). As he was about to find out, he had placed more faith in his own faith and unfailing love than in God Himself. However, Jesus was praying for Peter's faith (Luke 22:32). Peter quickly fell into the lowest valley of his life, denying Jesus in front of a group of servants. Peter was devastated. The dynamic of Peter's recovery is described in John 21. It is interesting that Jesus asked if Peter loved Him, using the word *agape*, the word for unconditional love, yet Peter could only say he loved Him as a brother, using the word *phileo*. At one time Peter thought his faith and love for Jesus were unconditional, but his trust in his own faith and love had been shattered. Now Jesus was moving Peter's faith onto a new foundation. In the masterful healing of Peter's spirit, Jesus reestablished Peter's faith in Him alone. He accepted all the love Peter could give, restored his call, and repeated the process three times, the same number of times Peter denied him. The healing went as deep as the wound. Then—in one of those strange ways Jesus had of comforting people—He told Peter how he would die for Him (John 21:18-19). These strange words were actually the culmination of Peter's healing. After he had denied Jesus in front of "nobodies," Peter could no longer even imagine that he would die for Him. That had become as unthinkable as moving a mountain. Jesus' prophetic word was the final piece in His restoration of Peter—Peter's faith would be strong.

The results of this pruning and subsequent restoration were astounding. Peter's greatest failure became his greatest strength. Next we see Peter, the same man who denied knowing Jesus in front of servants, preaching the sermon to the crowd at Pentecost and later risking his life by witnessing the truth of Jesus before the highest council in all Israel. Because so much of his writing in Scripture was advice to the persecuted church, scholars have dubbed him, "Apostle to the Persecuted." And when he was about to be killed for his faith, tradition records that he was crucified upside down, saying that he was not worthy to die a death like His Master's, to whom he owed everything. When it came to faith, Peter had to travel through the valley before he could climb to the heights.

> **In the masterful healing of Peter's spirit, Jesus reestablished Peter's faith in Him alone.**

I once heard a prophetic individual speak about a vision he had of a crowded stadium. The Lord was powerfully present, healing countless people and even bringing the dead back to life. Yet the meeting did not involve speakers with recognizable names. Nameless people spoke and ministered among the attendees. In this vision, a miracle occurred somewhere in the crowd and reporters came running up to those who had been praying. They asked, "What is your name?" But those praying refused to answer, saying that their names were not important; they were only servants of Jesus. Such humility struck me—how could anyone be so humble that they wouldn't even mention their name? I could not imagine attaining such humility. Then I realized that after stumbling around and walking through our own valleys long enough—discovering nothing within ourselves to brag about—that when God does choose to use us, we will be thoroughly convinced that God alone deserves all the credit. There may be valleys, but those who are obedient to walk through them God will lift up to walk in remarkable heights.

Believing *For* and Hope

We believe *in* God. But there is also a believing *for*. We believe *for* things. Those things are the objects of our faith. The biblical term for what we believe *for* is *hope* (See Hebrews 11:1). We believe for salvation—that is our certain hope. God gives us other things to believe for. Maybe He will tell us to have faith for a certain person to be healed or to come to salvation. Whatever we apply our faith to is our hope. What we believe *in* is easy: God. What to believe *for*, our hope, is a much harder question to answer.

> **What we believe *in* is easy: God.
> What to believe *for*, our hope, is a much
> harder question to answer.**

We cannot fail to believe for things. We must dream and hope. Sometimes—when we've set our hope on something and it was dashed—it is easier to resolve, "I'm not going to hope in anything ever again. If I don't hope, I will never be disappointed, and life will be much easier." But God will not allow us to go that route. Scripture says, "Without a vision the people perish" (Prov. 29:18). We have to dream. It's the only way to live. At the same time, however, we must believe for the right thing. What we hope for must be God's idea. Again, it gets back to seeing and knowing what the Father is doing. It's finding out what is His idea and what is not. If what we believe for is own our idea and not His, we are in presumption and not faith. Our hope is not accurate.

Even if He says to hope in something and we interpret it our own way or add our own thinking to it—things which are easy to do—we can get into presumption and may end up hurt or disappointed. It's like the old joke about the man caught in a flood. Trapped by the rising waters, he heard the Lord tell him that He would save him. So he climbed up on his porch, then onto the roof, then onto the peak of his roof. A boat went by and the people asked if he wanted to get in. He said, "No, God is going to save me." Another boat came by and he said the same thing. Finally a helicopter flew by, but again he refused help, "No thanks, God is going to save me." Finally he drowned. When he went to heaven, he told God, "I thought you were going to save me!" God said, "I sent two boats and a helicopter. What more did you want?"

That is an old, worn-out joke, but it illustrates how we can go wrong by interpreting His ideas in our own way— sometimes it can lead to disastrous consequences. We need to be accurate. We need to know what God is telling us to hope for and how to interpret that hope. Sometimes He tells us exactly what we are to believe for. Salvation is such a hope, solidly spelled out in His Word—we can believe for it without question. But in other situations, like praying for a sick person, although we know that healing is God's will in general, we may not know specifically how or when. What do we do then? Before I answer that question, let me give an example of a time when He did tell me specifically what to hope for.

The Battle of Faith

In 1990 I received a phone call from my mother. She said that my father had become seriously ill. It looked like a stroke, but later we found out it was viral encephalitis. I set out on the eight-hour drive to my parents' home in northern Michigan. Before I left, I felt the Lord telling me as I prayed, "This time he's going to come through, but there will be a time when things will be different." I held that in mind as the miles rolled by.

When I got there, things looked very bad. He had fallen into a deep coma and the doctors were thinking about removing the respirator, doubting he would make it though the night. That evening I asked God, "What should I do? How should I pray? What are You doing?"

That night I remember God saying, "This is a battle of faith. Remember what I told you. Go back and battle it out."

Once I heard that, I went back the next morning and battled with faith. Oddly, my sister had heard Him say the same thing. I spoke to Dad with words of faith. "Dad, you're a fighter. God is on your side. He wants you to pull through. Go for it. I'm with you and God is with you. He's going to help you go for it." I spoke faith to him and prayed over him again and again. It was a long ordeal, but all that happened was just as the words I had heard. Those critical days called for a battle of faith.

That time God graciously told me what would happen and helped me know how to pray. However, sometimes we just don't know what is going to happen or what to believe for. All we know is that God is good and always does good things. What do we do then? I say, if God doesn't tell you otherwise, be a fighter. He loves fighters (1 Tim. 6:12). Go in there and fight, knowing that good things happen as His kingdom comes. Sometimes all you know to pray is, "Holy Spirit, come. Fill this place and do all You want to do. We welcome Your mission and Your ministry here." Sometimes that is all we can do. But that's still hope, as accurate as we can get. And it's a faith that can apprehend mighty works.

> **Although God may tell you what He is going to do before the ministry session, sometimes He waits, showing you what He is doing *during* ministry, as He is doing it.**

Although God may tell you what He is going to do before the ministry session, sometimes He waits, showing you what He is doing *during* ministry, as He is doing it. Often His presence, His voice and His works come to us almost simultaneously. I have found it is best to be comfortable with not knowing exactly what He is going to do and simply watch Him do it. This involves a faith in *Him* rather than a faith dependent upon our knowing everything He is going to do. It may seem a little scary at first, but it is a fascinating, productive and thrilling way of ministering.

The Author of Our Faith

Faith comes from God. This is an interesting, perhaps obvious statement that has powerful implications. It says in Hebrews 12:2, "Let us fix our eyes on Jesus, the author and perfecter of our faith." He is the One who gives faith. Often we find ourselves in a situation where we know that faith is vital, but we feel that faith is something we need to drum up within ourselves in order for God to act. That can put enormous pressure on us. The more we try, the harder it is to find that faith. In reality, we do not "drum it up." He is the source, and we will be far more effective if we know that.

Sometimes the sheer emotion of desperately wanting something from God—like a loved one to be healed—can put this unproductive where-is-my-faith pressure on us. Sometimes those being prayed for can put this pressure on themselves, feeling it is their fault or that they will disappoint us if nothing happens. Sometimes, if a person has received prayer without results, a hopelessness and sense of failure can arise that brings more of this unproductive pressure into play. Because this is so common, it is sometimes easier to pray for an unbeliever who doesn't know what to expect than a believer who puts himself or herself under this pressure. However, these pressures can be dealt with if you recognize them and put the person's eyes in the right place.

In the 1940's God was doing remarkable things through many different healing ministries. One ministry in particular, that of Charles Price, saw an amazingly high number of healings. It was often said that if a person could not find healing anywhere else, he or she could go to Price's meetings and be healed. The premise of his ministry, spelled out in his book, *The Real Faith*, is that faith is not something that we drum up, but is something that God gives us when His presence comes. Many who had been unsuccessfully prayed for before were worried and filled with thoughts like, "I must not have enough faith." To those who were under this condemnation and pressure, Price would say in essence, "Don't worry about it. When God shows up, He will give you faith." Price always put the focus on God and His presence, which came in a powerful way. Price's tremendous track record for healings was based upon the simple but powerful premise: God gives us faith! When God's presence comes, faith comes.

> **Price's tremendous track record for healings was based upon the simple but powerful premise: God gives us faith! When God's presence comes, faith comes.**

While it is true that faith is something we can cultivate, we cannot manufacture it. As the author, God gives faith, and as the perfecter, He gives us more faith. (Hebrews 12:2) Sometimes I do ask God for faith, just as I ask Him for any other gift. Primarily, though, I am seeking Him and His presence, knowing He will give what I need when I need it.

Where Our Faith Resides

It says in Hebrews 11:1, "Faith is the substance of things hoped for, the evidence of things not seen." (KJV) Although the word *substance* is not literal but only implied in the Greek, I like that word and think of faith as a spiritual substance. It is a substance which resides not so much in our minds as in our spirits. Although it can come through the mind via hearing, as described in Romans 10:17, it primarily lives in our spirits. As we read about God's exploits in the Word or hear about His works from the experience of other people, our mind is involved in hearing. But that is not enough. It must affect us and sink into our spirits.

It is important to realize this because sometimes we can think that we have faith when we don't. (This is one cause for pruning.) At other times, we may think we don't have faith but we really do. Often we underestimate our faith: when our minds run out of ideas, solutions and answers, we can think that we don't have any faith, only to discover that true faith resides deep within. It can be greatly encouraging to find out that, just when we thought we were all out, we do have faith after all.

Several years ago I was high up in the southern Rocky Mountains in New Mexico. On my last day, as I was making my way back to my car, a strong wind was whipping up sand and blowing it into my face. One of those grains of sand blew right into my eye. I was wearing contact lenses, so the smallest grain of sand in my eye felt like a rock. This one felt huge.

As I was blinking in pain with tears running down my cheek, I debated whether I should take my lens out and risk losing it in the wind or endure the pain even longer. I really could not afford to lose it—I had a drive of almost fourteen hundred miles ahead of me and couldn't imagine driving it one-eyed. As I walked, the grain of sand kept feeling bigger and bigger, inflicting more and more pain.

Finally all I could think of was the relief of taking the lens out. I decided to take it out very carefully and hold it in my hand.

I cautiously popped the lens out of my eye and caught it in my cupped hand. Just to be sure, I peeked in my hand to see if it was there. But no sooner did I see it than the wind blew it out of my hand and it was gone! I saw it fly through the air and estimated about where it had landed—in the middle of an area where three sidewalks met to form a triangular patch, about 20 x 20 x 20 feet. The patch was filled with gravel. Unfortunately for me, the gravel in that part of the country contained tiny, shiny specks, each one glistening in the sun like a contact lens!

Since I was experimenting with my unusual approach to faith in those days, I saw this as an opportunity to exercise my incredible faith. "A challenge! God is going to show me where my contact lens is!" I felt quite confident that He was going to do just that. (A good example of mental conviction!) I prayed, "God, You can show me where it is. I'm going to do all the things I know I should do and I'm going to find that lens." So I started looking, walking all around the patch of gravel and quoting every Scripture I could remember— although I couldn't find too many that had to do with contact lenses. After about five minutes, I started to say, "God, I know that You know all things. You are all powerful. You are omniscient. You know everything. You know exactly where that lens is. The problem is, I don't. And it would be a *very* simple thing for You to tell me where it is."

I looked for another five minutes and still hadn't found it. I was getting a little desperate. I started saying, "God, what's wrong here? I know Your promises. I know that You'll help us in our time of need. This is my time of need and I need Your help. I know You can do it."

Another five minutes went by and I was getting more and more upset and frustrated. I started saying things like, "God, I want to be honest with You. I'm feeling a little disappointed here. If I can't have faith for a little thing like this, how am I going to do the big exploits I know You want us to do?"

Finally, after twenty or twenty-five minutes, I came to the end of my faith barrel. I was scraping around for just a few dregs but finding nothing much. "Lord, I am really disappointed here. I don't know if I can trust You to do things anymore, because I know how easy it would be for You to do this. I know You want to help me. Where are You?" Resigned, after praying all these inspiring prayers, I was in a desperate place.

The amazing thing was, after all this, I found myself saying, "But, You know, Lord, I don't know why, but I will still follow You all the days of my life. I could never let go of You."

Now the story didn't have to end this way, but it did. Having said that, I stooped down just one more time, reached out in front of me and picked up the contact lens. There it was.

Then I remembered all I had said. I looked up and said, "God, I am so embarrassed about the things I said. I'm sorry."

I heard Him answer me—not an audible voice, but one that I knew was His, "You know, that was the longest we've talked in quite a while! I liked that!" He added, "Wasn't it interesting that, even when you thought your faith had run out, you could not let go of Me?"

I thought again, "That's true, I could not let go of You."

And I heard Him say, "I want to show you what true faith is all about. True faith resides in your spirit. It's like a rope that connects you to Me, your heart to My heart. That rope cannot give way. It will never let go. *That* is true faith. Even when you think you are at the bottom of your supply of faith, this true faith will not let go." I've never forgotten that. I've been through much harder experiences, but I know that this substance, this true faith that God has authored, is much deeper and much stronger than we can think or imagine.

What we think is the bottom of our well is not the bottom at all. Our well is connected to God's well and His well runs infinitely deep. He wants to pour His well into ours, giving us more and more.

When my father was sick, in the days of battle, I would go home at night feeling that my well was very nearly dry. I had been with my dad all day, praying with all I had, and I felt I had no more left to give. At night when the phone would ring, I would jump. I can only refer to it as the "terror of the telephone" because it was such a loud ring and the hospital was supposed to call if anything happened. As I would fall asleep, I would wonder if I had the faith to go on for another day. But the next morning I would wake up and find that the Lord had filled my well. I was filled with faith again. Each night I would feel empty, and each morning my well would again be filled. I have learned from experiences like this that God is faithful—He is faith-*full*, and that when He comes, He brings faith itself with Him, all that we need. Put your well to His and let Him pour.

> **Our well is connected to God's well and His well runs infinitely deep.**

Fear

Faith is the opposite of fear. After years of observing and ministering to people, both inside and outside the church, I've become convinced that fear is one of the most damaging emotions people can have within. It is at the root of many other maladies that can affect a person. It is also at the root of many of society's maladies, such as prejudice and hysteria. John F. Kennedy felt that the two most dangerous qualities a world leader could have were fear and pride. I am convinced that more damage has been done within the church because of fear than anything else. It promulgates competition, slander, division, rigidness and isolationism. If anyone is called to walk in faith, it is the church.

One of the most deadly forms of individual fear is insecurity—deadly because it is a hidden fear. Insecurity can masquerade as humility, but it is not. Insecurity and pride are actually two sides of the same coin, arising from the fear of man. The "golden" coin they mimic is humility and boldness, arising from the true fear of God. They are very different coins. Behind insecurity is the fear of something, whether it is fear of failure, pain, losing friends, or losing acceptance. Whatever our fears, with God's enabling power we must identify them, pull out our sword, and slay them ruthlessly. Put those fears in the cross hairs and pull the trigger. I'm sorry for the violent analogies, but you must slay them before they slay you!

> **Whatever our fears, with God's enabling power we must identify them, pull out our sword, and slay them ruthlessly.**

Applications for Team Ministry

There are some things you can do to help you minister in more true faith. There are also some things that will help you impart faith and hope to those for whom you pray.

How to Minister with Faith

• Don't "rev up" to try to produce faith. That is counter-productive. Instead relax and enjoy God. Worship Him, quote Scripture, or do whatever brings you into His presence.

• Let faith "come" on you—just as His presence comes on you. Faith and anointing (God's presence) go hand in hand.

• For your personal walk with the Lord, don't operate out of self-pity—the attitude that says, "If I get into a little more of this sad condition, maybe God will feel sorry for me and do something." That attitude simply doesn't work!

• Realize that God's mission and ministry cannot be stopped! If people, Satan, the entire Roman government, and even death could not stop the ministry of Jesus, do you really think that you, your inabilities or circumstances can stop Him?

• Ask for God's presence and for Him to pour His well of faith on you, that you may see the reality He sees—His promises and all that He is.

How to Minister Faith to Others

• Just as you should not "rev up" faith, don't try to get others to rev it up either. If you sense that others feel a pressure to produce faith, encourage them to relax and enjoy God. One of my friends would tell people that receiving prayer ministry is like being on a beach where all they have to do is lie back and enjoy the sunshine. (Granted this is not a parable from the Bible, but it is fairly analogous to the approach to take.)

• Although faith is important, it is not imparted to others by telling them they don't have it. (It is surprising how often this happens.) Faith comes by hearing about God and His exploits in Scripture, in your life, and in the testimonies of others—not by hearing that they are a failure in everything including having faith!

• Learn to recognize when the Spirit is on a person and when they have faith. (See Acts 14:9.) That's when you can go forward. Learn to recognize feelings of fear, unworthiness or worry that nothing will happen. Sometimes body language can give this away. (When you see negative posture, sometimes it can be helpful for the person to change the position of their body. Somehow, a more positive body position can help break a negative mental position.) If you see anything like this that is blocking ministry, address that first. Ask God and He will show you how.

How to Minister Hope to Others

• Remember that hope is an essential part of faith. Those without a vision perish (Prov. 29:18). Hopelessness is a devastating condition that usually blocks any other healing. It is the enemy's work in a person's life—hopelessness is his "crowning glory" to nail shut the door on his victim's pain. It usually manifests itself as a fatalistic attitude: "Nothing is going to happen. Nothing will do any good." Minister to that first! Hopelessness affects a person's demeanor and enthusiasm for life; it brings discouragement and depression. But the Lord knows how to break through! I have seen Him reveal to the ministry team the very words that originally instilled hopelessness in the person and then reverse those words and bring a wellspring of hope in their place.

• Be sure that the people have an accurate hope. Creating inaccurate hope, by saying what people want to hear but not what God is saying, can increase short-term "faith" and happiness at the expense of long-term hope and wellbeing. Accurate hope takes into account the trials that may accompany a promise of God. Joseph, Moses and many others who were given incredible promises by God, then went through some of the worst wilderness experiences imaginable before they saw their promises fulfilled. Their trials did not mean that God was unhappy, finished with them, or that they had done something wrong. Their trials came *because* His promises were true. Trials can come both from God, who is trying to help us—sometimes by killing our flesh—and from the enemy, who is trying to kill our spirits. The enemy may see the promises on our life even when we cannot and is threatened by them. We must tell people this and encourage them in the reality of an accurate hope so that their faith is not shaken by the bumps and problems that come along the way.

• Let God's light shine on people. His light produces hope. Often, as you minister, God will tell you about the dreams and promises He has given others. These precious people and their visions must not perish! The world around us constantly drains our hope and encouragement. One function of the prophetic gifts is to speak God's hopes back into people (1 Cor. 14:3). Have you ever received a word that was so encouraging it strengthened you to go on for miles? Can you imagine what it would be like if—instead of cutting each other down—everyone in the church was sensitive enough to the Lord to give words of encouragement to one another? People would have the strength and courage to go the distance. The church would be mobilized! We desperately need the ministry of encouragement. Imparting hope, accurate hope, is one of the central things we, as ministry team members, are called to do.

God's presence is what we are after, giving us everything we need, even faith itself. Walk in that faith, revel in it. Be people of faith, courage and perseverance. When Jesus returns, will He find faith on earth? His eyes are looking to and fro even now, looking for those He may use for His awesome works.

6

Shifting Our Paradigms: I'll See It When I Believe It

A few years ago the teens in our church befriended a young man named Danny. Danny spent most of his time on the streets. A severe head injury as an infant had affected him mentally. One of his endearing qualities was the way he would quote cliches—usually a little mixed up. For instance, "I'll believe it when I see it," would always come out as "I'll see it when I believe it." We loved that because we realized that with the things of God, Danny's words were much closer to the truth.

It seems that some people, even Christians, do not believe that God works supernaturally today like He did in the Book of Acts. Their experience seems to confirm their belief—they do not see supernatural acts. Others believe that He does do supernatural things today and do see them happening. How do you explain this disparity? I think two factors are at play. First, faith is a requirement for receiving from God, so even though some may believe God for salvation and receive it, they may not believe Him for supernatural acts and therefore do not experience them. Second, a lack of belief in something can actually affect what we see and hear. (See John 12:29)

Supernatural activity can be going on in front of us but, unless we are attuned to it, we can dismiss it before it registers in our minds.

Paradigms and World Views

Our belief system affects the way we view the world, influencing what we "see" and don't see. In other words, our *paradigm*—the way we model the world in our minds and believe it works—affects our *worldview*—the way we "see" things. I put "see" in quotes because our eyes actually see everything around us, but the complexity of images that come at us are preprocessed by our minds so that we can concentrate only on what we think is important. For instance, when we drive a car, we may not notice the different shades of gray in the pavement ahead of us because we have learned that they are not important. That information is filtered out at a low level in our seeing process so that other information, such as a child playing near the street, can attract our mind's fuller attention. When someone from the South moves to the colder climates, however, the first time they hit a patch of ice on the road they may be in for a *paradigm shift*: they had not realized that the subtle shades of gray in the road's appearance were meaningful and did not really "see" the icy patches in the road ahead. When they realize how important those variations on the roadway can be, they suddenly start seeing those different colored patches. Their paradigm shifted, affecting the way they view the world.

Another good example of a paradigm shift occurred when I began shopping for a particular make of automobile. Before I became interested in purchasing a Saturn, I could have sworn that I had never seen very many of them on the road. Once I became interested in them, however, it was amazing how many I began to see! Although I previously believed that Saturns existed, I did not feel they were very important. When my paradigm shifted my view of the world changed. The same is true of the supernatural acts of God. God can speak to us prophetically, but if we are not attuned to the fact that He might speak to us like that today, we can dismiss His thoughts before they even enter our minds. Or, if they do enter our minds, we might just attribute them to insight and not give them another thought. The variety of ways the Father can show us what He is doing, as discussed in previous chapters, can also be dismissed if they are not part of our paradigm. Even miracles can be missed by those without the paradigms and, therefore, the worldviews to see them.

> **God can speak to us prophetically, but if we are not attuned to the fact that He might speak to us like that today, we can dismiss His thoughts before they even enter our minds.**

Sometimes merely hearing someone talk about the extraordinary ways God operates is enough to begin shifting our paradigms. Then the more open we become to "seeing" what God is doing, the more we actually begin to see a new view of the world. Then, in turn, the new things we see excite us and shift our paradigms even more. Those things we now see are, and always have been, real, but now our eyes are opened and we are more fully aware of the diverse ways God acts.

The Shifting Paradigms in Mark

While the word "paradigm" is not found in Scripture, the Gospel of Mark is filled with dramatic examples of paradigm shifts and changing world views. The Book of Mark is a short, action-oriented account of the ministry of Jesus. Most of the verbs in the original Greek are in the present tense and get the reader "caught up" in the action and experience of being with Jesus. Because of the immediacy of the text, it is easy to put ourselves in the shoes of the people as they reacted to all that was said and done. Their reactions can be viewed as a progression, which Mark often describes through variations of the word *amazed*. While *amazed* may be connected with the people's emotional state of mind, Mark uses it to point us to the radical underlying change in the way the people thought about God and the world—radical shifts in their paradigms! For the reader, Mark's intent (and God's!) is for *our* eyes to be opened, for our paradigms to shift, and in the process, for our expectant faith to grow. At one point, Jesus, frustrated that the disciples still had their old mind-sets even after seeing many miracles, said, "Do you have eyes but fail to see, and ears but fail to hear?" (Mark 8:18). His intent is that we would see and therefore believe—and believe and therefore see!

If you look up *amazed* in the *Englishman's Greek Concordance* (the index will point you to *amazed* and all its synonyms), you will find fourteen occurrences in the Book of Mark. (This, by the way, makes an outstanding group Bible study!) Placing them in the order they occur, the forms of the word *amazed* (as shown by the words of their English translations) increase in intensity. (Note: I would like to thank Prof. Louis Brighton not only for giving me a love for the Book of Mark, but also for laying a thorough groundwork on how Mark used the word *amazed*.)

In Mark 1:22 they were *amazed* at Jesus' words. In Mark 1:27 and 2:12 they were *amazed* at His works. In Mark 5:42 they were "completely astonished" (NIV) or "astonished with a great astonishment" (KJV) at His raising a girl from the dead. In Mark 6:2 they were *amazed* at His wisdom, and in 6:51 were "completely amazed" (NIV) or "sore amazed" (KJV) at His walking on water. In Mark 7:37 they were "overwhelmed with amazement" (NIV) or "beyond measure astonished" (KJV) at a miraculous healing. (Three more instances in Mark 10, surrounding the meeting with the rich young ruler, are discussed in a later chapter.)

Mark 9:15 contains the most intensive form of *amazed* in Biblical Greek (found only in the Book of Mark). Just after the Transfiguration, Jesus approached a crowd gathered around His disciples who had failed to cast out a dumb spirit from a man's son. As the crowd saw Jesus, they were "overwhelmed with wonder" (NIV), although they had not yet seen Him do anything or heard Him say a word. Why such an intensive form of *amazed* when nothing had happened? Some have speculated that He was glowing from the Transfiguration, but Scripture does not say this. It only says they saw Him. I believe their paradigms had been shifted with each act and word of Jesus that they had previously experienced. Now Jesus did not have to do or say anything to cause their expectancy to surge—He only needed to be seen. This is where Mark is trying to take us. When, in their desperation, they suddenly saw Jesus walking toward them, they now had eyes to see that He was all they needed. "Jesus is here! Anything can happen!" So it is with us as we progress in the shifting of our paradigms and the growth of our faith. We learn by experience who Jesus is and what awesome things can happen when He comes.

"Jesus is here! Anything can happen!"

The action-packed part of Mark ends with Mark 16:8. It is followed by a twelve-verse epilog written in a separate style. The change in style sets the epilog apart from the rest of the book. Therefore, imagine a long pause as the original hearers are left hanging with the emotion of what they heard as Mark 16:8 ends. The stone is rolled away, an angel says "Jesus is risen" and then "Trembling and bewildered, the women went out and fled from the tomb. They said nothing to anyone, because they were afraid." (NIV) This intensive form of amazed (translated *afraid* in the NIV) is so intense that it has an element of fear and bewilderment. Some scholars wonder how Mark could end on a note of fear, but I believe this was not ordinary fear but the apex, the culmination of the amazement of what the people had experienced—the ultimate in paradigm shifts as they saw the empty tomb. As the disciples saw the tomb's emptiness, their jaws dropped as if to say, "If He is not here, where is He?!" If the reader's attitude in Mark 9:15 was, "Jesus is here! Anything can happen!" now it had become, "Now He could be *anywhere* and come at any time!" Mark, in fact, leaves us with faith for the era in which we now live. By God's presence, He now *can* be anywhere and come at any time! We are left astonished, our paradigms shifted and our world view now ready and expecting the amazing works of the kingdom to happen at any time.

Faith and Risk

For our paradigms to shift, we have to experience something new. That involves risk. Faith, by its nature, always involves risk. To walk the walk of faith we must constantly take risks. In the story of the servant who buried his master's money to keep it safe, the master, when he returned, was furious that the servant had not taken a risk. The moral of this story is that when it comes to God, it is riskier *not* to take a risk than it is to take one! The heroes of faith mentioned in Hebrews 11 all had this in common; they were risk-takers. Even society's modern-day heroes tend to be people who have taken risks. But we are not supposed to just admire people like this—we are supposed to *be* a people who take risks ourselves.

The first time I watched *Braveheart*, I was impacted not only by the movie but also by what the Lord highlighted and spoke to me as I watched it. (He can draw lessons out of any life experience.) At the movie's end I felt the words came into my mind, "If this is going to be the land of the free, then the church is going to have to be the home of the brave." We live in a world and generation that needs faith desperately. With some notable exceptions, the church today is often more motivated by fear and its by-products than by faith. The lack of faith even shades the way we look at Scripture. We often think of Peter as being the one who sank in the sea, but he was the only one besides Jesus who ever walked on water! God loves the heart that takes risks. We identify with Thomas as the one who doubted. But he didn't stay that way. His life ended when he was shot with an arrow while praying. It takes faith to pray, even more when it places your life in danger. If we think, when we get to heaven, that we will see Thomas as a doubting, lowly figure, we are mistaken! Tens of thousands of Syrians will be thanking God for him and seeing him as a man of tremendous faith—a risk-taker who traveled to their country and founded the Syrian church. Jesus asks our generation what He asked in Luke 18:8, "When the Son of Man comes, will He find faith on earth?" We must respond to that challenge. We must be a people of faith.

In many different ways we must take risks and overcome. We must risk the chance of failing. Do you know which baseball player struck out more than anyone in his time? It was Babe Ruth, the same one who set the home run record. If he had not risked failing, he could not have succeeded in doing what he did.

We must take risks in ministry settings. Moving out in a spiritual gift or praying for someone for the first time seems like a huge risk. In teaching people how to minister, one of John Wimber's favorite sayings was, "Faith is spelled R-I-S-K." For me, the things we do in ministry still sometimes seem like a risk. But it is always a risk worth taking.

Even coming closer to God may seem like a huge risk. Consider Moses, who risked his life to come to God in the burning bush on the mountain! We do not know what will happen to us when we come to His presence. When a person comes to salvation it may seem a big risk, and it may seem like a risk as we place our lives in His hands to do with as He pleases.

Sometimes the risk God is calling us to take is to change the direction of our life. Other times it is to stick with what we are doing. Often we must risk looking foolish. We must risk coming out of our comfort zone. We must risk experiencing the new. It is often like jumping off a diving board—it's scary on the climb up, it's scary when we jump off, but once we're in the water the feeling is great.

If we are to bring our ministry outside the four walls of the church, that, too, will probably feel risky and uncomfortable at first. But once we have grown in this ministry and developed a love and sensitivity for people and for God, we will simply have to push through our resistance towards taking risks and go for it.

Valor and Perseverance

Scripture uses different words to describe different types of faith (and risk-taking) for different types of situations. Valor is faith in the face of battle. During *Braveheart*, in the scene before William Wallace died, he prayed, "I am so afraid. Let me die well." At first that struck me as odd; this man of uncommon bravery said he was afraid. I felt the Lord telling me, "Being brave doesn't mean that you are never afraid. It means that your cause burns in your heart and controls your life more than your fear." We need the cause of Christ to burn in us so intensely that, no matter what we are called to do, His cause—and we—will go forward.

In some ways we can prepare to exercise valor before opportunities which call for valor come. Rudolph Giuliani, the former mayor of New York City, is noted for his courage under fire as he piloted his city through the 9/11 crisis. Years before 2001, he studied the heroism of Winston Churchill during the bombing of Britain and the way Churchill led his country through those perilous times. When the crisis hit New York, Giuliani knew what to do. Thinking about how we might respond to certain situations can help us prepare. We need not be in the midst of war when an opportunity to exercise valor comes; it may be just helping someone in need. This may sound much easier than facing an actual battle, but such opportunities are all too easy to miss. One problem is that they usually come at unexpected—and inconvenient—times. It is too easy to continue on with our plans for the day and perhaps not even see these opportunities. If we can more frequently ask the Father to show us what He is doing, we can spend less time engrossed in our busy schedule and more time open to what God might show us. Sometimes we need to purposefully push open our worldview beyond the unrelenting pace of our lives so that we can see what God is doing.

Perseverance is faith in the face of repeated danger and failure. We must not let failure defeat us; instead, we must let it increase our resolve to succeed. Rick Joyner wrote an example of one man's life which exemplified this principle in his book *Leadership, Management and the Five Essentials for Success*.

1831	He failed in business
1832	He was defeated for the Legislature
1833	He failed again in business
1836	He suffered a nervous breakdown
1838	He was defeated for Speaker of the Legislature
1840	He was defeated for Elector
1843	He was defeated for Congress
1848	He was defeated again for Congress
1855	He was defeated for the Senate
1856	He was defeated for Vice President
1858	He was defeated for the Senate again
1860	He was elected President
	He preserved the Union

Of course, he was writing about Abraham Lincoln. Joyner goes on to write, "It is hard to comprehend how a human being could endure the continual crises and pressures Abraham Lincoln suffered while president. The list above explains such endurance. . . . *Every defeat made Lincoln more determined and more prepared for his ultimate task.*" (Excerpted from page 87 of *Leadership, Management and the Five Essentials for Success.* Copyright ©1990 by Rick Joyner. Used by permission of MorningStar Publications. For more information see: www.morningstarministries.org.)

We must let defeat make us better, not bitter, and more determined and prepared for our task ahead.

Helps to Minister Paradigm Shifts

We need to realize that change, unfamiliar styles of ministry and anything unknown can be a culture shock to many people. Therefore, when praying for others or when presenting this material, you may run into two types of people: those who like and even thrive on adventure and new experiences, and those who are more cautious and even afraid.

There are possible pitfalls for both these groups. The adventurous can chase thrills at the expense of cultivating character and intimacy. The cautious or fearful can reject or become isolated from new experiences that are essential for growing in the Lord. The following tips will be helpful in avoiding both kinds of pitfalls.

• Don't put out the enthusiasm of the first group (a precious resource!) or dampen the sensitivity of the second. Be open; share how you struggled to get past your own paradigm barriers—the stories are usually funny, give the first group more sensitivity and make the second group feel they are not alone, giving hope that they, too, can break through.

• If you talk about God, His wonders, intimacy with Him, developing character and helping others, you will bring both types of people to where they should be.

• If you love the people and touch them where they need healing, even the most timid will allow God in and appreciate the ways He can work. That's what Jesus did!

• Sharing personal experiences helps to whet people's appetites to learn more. Allow others to share their experiences. For every person who shares, there is usually a listener whose life will be affected by the story. Testimonies build faith.

• Allow people's hunger to drive them to search the Scriptures for themselves. It is how every mighty man or woman of God began their journey. It's in the Book, but hunger has to motivate their own exploring. As eyes open and paradigms shift, the new "world view" will bring a new view of the Bible itself, seeing verses that were always there but never given much attention nor understood. Then, eyes will see the new truth in everyday life. As Danny said, "I'll see it when I believe it."

7
Authority

Two interesting words in the New Testament are *exousia*, the Greek word for authority, and *dunamis*, the Greek word for power (from which we get the word dynamite). To explain the difference, consider a policeman. His weapons are his *dunamis*; his badge is his *exousia*. Even though he occasionally might use, or threaten to use, his gun, it is really his badge—his authority—that is most effective in enforcing what he says. If you choose to disobey him, you might be able to run from him and avoid his weaponry, but if he knows who you are and where you live, he could bring the entire force of the city, state or nation down upon you. So you obey!

Another example is found in the Army. There are times when weaponry, *dunamis*, makes a soldier effective. But, even armed with the most sophisticated weapons, if you, as a soldier, went into the enemy's camp, walked up to the commander and, weapons in hand, demanded he surrender, he would probably laugh in your face because there would be one of you compared to his thousands. If, on the other hand, he looked over your shoulder and saw an army of millions behind you, and he knew that you demanded his surrender in the authority of that army, your words would carry a lot of weight. That's authority—*exousia*.

In ministry, both power and authority are effective and essential tools. To be fully equipped, it is necessary to understand and use them both. Authority comes from who Jesus says we are and whom we represent. Power comes from the Holy Spirit flowing in and through us. It is really God being with us that gives us both. However, it is still useful to separate the concepts of power and authority to learn more about them.

God is calling us to walk in authority. Jesus did. When He spoke, everybody knew He had it. And, through Scripture, He teaches us the amazing fact that we, too, have authority and shows us how to use it.

Authority and Relationship

The first key to understand is that to be *in* authority, we must be *under* authority. Even Jesus said, "I only do what I see the Father doing" (John 5:19). Even though, being God, He could have had authority in and of Himself, it says in Philippians 2 that He became a servant and walked under the authority of His Father. He modeled how we are to walk—in and under God's authority and in the power of the Holy Spirit. Walking in the Father's authority went hand in hand with being in continual relationship with His Father. At the very beginning of Jesus' ministry, when He was baptized by John the Baptist, the Father spoke from heaven, saying, "You are My Son . . ." Relationship was the beginning of Jesus' authority and ministry and it must be the beginning of ours.

Since this authority is connected with relationship, it is a different kind of authority than we see in the world. The people in Jesus' day knew He was different. He spoke with authority, not as the Scribes spoke (Mark 1:22). It was not authoritarianism, an arrogant attitude, a superficial pretense, or a use of smooth and flashy words, but true spiritual authority. In true authority the power comes from God, not from men. With true authority, the more you realize you need God, the more you will walk with Him and, therefore, the more authority you will have.

Authority and the Sovereignty of God— a Stumbling Block in Our Understanding of Prayer

Dutch Sheets, in His book *Intercessory Prayer*, has some excellent insights about authority. I was particularly intrigued by a question he posed which he had pondered in his own life. "If God is sovereign, does prayer really make a difference?" We know for a fact that God is sovereign. And we also know that it does say in the Lord's prayer, "Your kingdom come, Your will be done," implying that we are supposed to ask for God's will to be done. The question remains, however, since God is sovereign, and His will is going to be done anyway, does it really make a difference whether or not we ask Him to do things? It was one of those questions, Dutch said, that he was almost afraid to ask God. When I read his question I knew that, deep down, I had the same question and, whether I verbalized it or not, that question really affected the frequency and intensity with which I prayed. If this question is somewhere within us, we may still pray, but it is easy to let prayer slip out of our lives— because there is a part of us that does not really believe it is necessary or would even do any good.

> **Since God is sovereign, and His will is going to be done anyway, does it really make a difference whether or not we ask Him to do things?**

One of the blessings of seeking God is that often, when you ask questions of Him, He will not only answer you but will also give you a gold mine of understanding. That was the case with Dutch's question as he sought God for an answer. What he found was so valuable that, in the next several pages, I will review some of his supporting Scriptures and the answer he found.

Let's start in the beginning. Genesis 1:26-28 reads, "Then God said, 'Let us make man in our image, in our likeness, and let them rule over the fish of the sea and the birds of the air, over the livestock, over all the earth, over all the creatures that move along the ground.' So God created man in His own image; in the image of God He created him; male and female He created them. God blessed them, and said, 'Be fruitful and increase in number; fill the earth and subdue it. Rule over the fish of the sea and the birds of the air and over every living creature that moves on the ground.'"

That is how God started everything. He gave humans the authority described here when essentially He said, "Go and rule over the earth, over the creation that I've made." Yes, God is sovereign, but in His sovereignty, He chose to give authority to us. Therein is the beginning of the answer, but let's expand upon it even further.

Psalm 8:3-8 agrees. "When I consider your heavens, the work of your fingers, the moon and the stars, which you have set in place, what is man that you are mindful of him, the son of man that you care for him? You made him a little lower than the heavenly beings and crowned him with glory and honor. You made him ruler over the works of your hands; you put everything under his feet: all flocks and herds, and the beasts of the field, the birds of the air, and the fish of the sea, all that swim the paths of the seas."

God has made human beings the ruler over the works of His hands. In His sovereignty, He has chosen to give this authority, this rulership, to us.

Psalm 115 again shows what God has given to man. Psalm 115:16: "The highest heavens belong to the Lord, but the earth He has given to man."

In the New Testament, we have another look at what God has given to man. In Luke 4:5-8, just after Jesus was baptized and went into the wilderness before beginning His ministry, we are told, "The devil led Him up to a high place and showed Him in an instant all the kingdoms of the world. And he said to Him, 'I will give You all their authority and splendor, for it has been given to me, and I can give it to anyone I want to. So if You worship me, it will all be Yours.' Jesus answered, 'It is written: 'Worship the Lord your God and serve him only.''"

Notice that Jesus, in responding to this, did not argue that what Satan said was true—that our authority on earth (at least in part) had been given to Satan. That happened by sin in the Garden of Eden.

That's not the end of the story, thankfully. Matthew 28:18 declares, "Jesus came up to them [after His death and resurrection] and said, 'All authority in heaven and on earth has been given to Me. Therefore go and make disciples of all nations . . .'" The authority—which started with us and fell into the hands of Satan—Jesus won back by His death on the cross. He took the keys from Satan. They are back in His hands!

When He tells us, "All authority has been given to Me on heaven and earth; therefore [*you*] go . . ." the implication is that Jesus is giving us authority, too. He wouldn't be telling us to "therefore go" if that were not true. It would be like me telling one of my children, "I have been given authority and power to stop crime. Now you go into the darkest part of the city and stop it." If I had the power and authority but they did not, it wouldn't make any sense to send my children. What this verse implies is that authority is now back in our hands again, too.

In Matthew 16:19, Jesus said, "On this rock I will build my church and the gates of hell will not overcome it. I give you the keys of the kingdom of heaven; whatever you bind on earth will be bound in heaven, whatever you loose on earth will be loosed in heaven." Here, in another way, He is saying that He has given us authority. We now have the keys, a symbol of authority, and, therefore, the ability to open every gate. This is reminiscent of Isaiah 22:22-23: "[I will] hand your authority over to him . . . I will place on his shoulder the key to the house of David; what he opens no one can shut, and what he shuts no one can open." The binding vs. loosing (and opening vs. shutting) are opposites and therefore all inclusive. The authority is ours to open the gates of heaven, unlock the prison doors, or close the gates of destruction over a person's life. If you think about it, virtually everything we might ask God to do either involves a separation (for example, a person and their sickness) or a bringing together, so Jesus words are very inclusive!

In another place He says, "If you forgive anyone his sins, they are forgiven; if you do not forgive them, they are not forgiven" (John 20:23). Again a separation. That's rather awesome! Even the Pharisees realized, "Who but God can forgive sins?" (Luke 5:21). But that authority is His, and even that authority He has given to His Church.

Often He tells us we may pray in His name. This is another way of saying that we may use His authority: whatever we ask or say will be taken by the Father as if Jesus were asking or saying it Himself. (The concept is similar to that of exercising power of attorney.)

> **Even though He is sovereign, Almighty God has chosen to partner with us.**

All of this is telling us that the sovereign God has *chosen* to give us authority and, therefore, will act in response to what we ask and do. This tells us that prayer *does* make a difference. Even though He is sovereign, Almighty God has chosen to partner with us. What we ask of Him He does, because He is in partnership with us. Of course, this does not mean that we can go and decide for Him what He should do, because this partnership works the way Jesus said it works in

John 5:19: "I only do what I see the Father doing." In other words, we have to be so close with the Lord that His heart beats within our heart, His will becomes our will.

God's Will Expressed in Our Words

As God shows us what His will is, that will needs to be expressed in prayer—in words. In His sovereignty, that's what He is looking for us to do. There is something powerful about expressing His will. Whether it is petitional prayer or speaking a prophetic word, it is spoken and then He moves. In creation, the word was spoken and then He acted—"Let there be light," and there was light.

Of course, we don't have to figure out every aspect of God's will before we can start to pray. Like David, we are constantly communicating with Him, friend to friend, and that is prayer. In the process, God allows His heart to be felt in ours. God, then, moves in response to what we ask. He has chosen to make us part of the process. That we are a part of it is mind-boggling and staggeringly awesome—but it is imperative that we know how it works.

An example of this is found in Daniel 10:12. Daniel had been praying and, Scripture says, the angel Gabriel was sent in response to his prayer. It actually took three weeks between Daniel's prayer and God's response. But when the angel arrived, he stated, "Your words were heard and I came in response to them." Daniel's prayer was heard and it brought God's action!

In James 4:2 it says, "You have not because you ask not." This clearly says that asking makes a difference. James 5:17-18 says that, "The prayer of a righteous man is powerful and effective. Elijah was a man just like us. He prayed earnestly that it would not rain and it did not rain on the land for three and a half years. Again he prayed, and the heavens gave rain, and the earth produced its crops." Elijah expressed the will of the Lord in words and God acted. We are told that we are just like Elijah; the things we ask in prayer the Lord will do.

Jesus, when teaching the disciples to pray, said, "Your will be done on earth as it is in heaven" (Matthew 6:10). Jesus taught that we are to express in words the desire that God's will be done. Our expression is a necessary step in the process of God's will being done on earth. The sovereign God has made it so.

Thus, there is a clear answer to the seeming conflict inherent in the question: if God is sovereign, does prayer really make a difference? God is sovereign, but He has chosen that prayer will make a difference. He has chosen that we partner with Him in the incredible move of His hands. (For Dutch Sheet's own discussion of his question and answer, see *Intercessory Prayer*, pp. 21-33.)

Types of Prayer For Team Ministry

In Chapter Three I mentioned three basic types of prayer: petition, intercession and prophetic prayer. Jesus Himself used all three. Building upon the foundational understanding of authority laid in this chapter, I can now go into more detail about each type of prayer, showing how effective each can be in ministry settings.

Petitional Prayer

Petitional prayer is simply asking God to do something. God is looking for those to do this. In Ezekiel 22:30-31 the Lord says, "I looked for a man among them who would build up the wall and stand before Me in the gap on behalf of the land so I would not have to destroy it, but I found none. So I will pour my wrath on them and consume them with my fiery anger, bringing on their own heads all they have done, declares the Sovereign Lord."

In this verse it almost looks as if there are two conflicting wills of the Lord: judgment and mercy. I would say, rather, that in judgment we reap the consequences of our sins. But, in the depth of God's heart, His desire is to somehow give mercy. In this verse He is looking for someone to express this cry of His heart for judgment to be replaced by mercy. When we pray for revival, that is exactly what we are praying for. One of the best definitions of revival is that mercy—His Spirit—is poured out in place of judgment. He is looking for those who will pray specifically this.

Some people look at America and say, "America deserves punishment. It is going to get what it deserves." It is true that America (or most any country) deserves judgment. But God is looking for people who have His heart, who cry for mercy and plead, "Oh God, give them another chance. Instead of judgment, won't You pour out Your Spirit? Won't You pour out revival?" He is looking for those who will feel this in their hearts and express it with their words. Whether we pray for an individual or for a nation, He's looking for those who will ask.

As we minister, realize that God is anxiously waiting for our request to pour out the riches of His heaven. Early in his ministry, just after experiencing his first success in praying for someone to be healed, John Wimber had a vision of a large honeycomb in the sky dripping with honey. When he asked what it was, God answered, "It is my mercy." He watched as some people reveled in it, others caught it in cups to give to others, and still others became thoroughly annoyed by the sticky mess of it all. God said, "It's My mercy, John. It is continually falling." It was a vision that constantly reminded John Wimber of God's will for healing. That is God's heart: to pour out the riches of heaven. So whether you are praying for a nation or for the individual standing in front of you, ask God to pour Himself upon them. God is looking for us to ask. "Ask and it will be given to you; seek and you will find; knock and the door will be opened to you . . . If you then, though you are evil, know how to give good gifts to your children, how much more will your Father in heaven give the Holy Spirit to those who ask Him!" (Luke 11:9,13).

Intercession

In the usual sense of the word, "intercession" does not mean "prayer." It really means taking on the role of mediator. Imagine two people having a major disagreement, each saying different things and not communicating, not understanding the position of the other person at all. If a third party comes into the room to hear each side and then explains the position of each person to the other, he would be acting as a mediator, or *intercessor*. He would be between the two parties, bringing each other's words to the other and, therefore, bringing the two people together.

Jesus acted as an intercessor—on God's behalf He showed us what God was like, expressing the will and nature of God and serving as His ambassador, reaching out to us with God's love. But He is also an intercessor on our behalf—He went before God for our sakes to reconcile us to God. He functioned on behalf of both parties—each estranged from the other (by sin)—and worked a mediation, a reconciliation, bringing them together.

In the Old Testament, the word for intercession is *paga*, the Hebrew word that is also the word for "meeting." As intercessors, we are to do the same thing that Jesus did. We are to bring both sides together in a meeting. We explain what God is like to the people—how much He loves them—and say to them, "Come, meet with the Lord." But we also bring the people before the Lord and ask the Lord to meet with them and minister. We are setting up the meeting between the people and the Lord.

Like many of my friends, I often used the phrase, "Come, Holy Spirit." One day I started thinking about this phrase and got to feeling that it sounded a bit audacious, like I was ordering Him around: "Holy Spirit, You come here right now!" I thought, "Who am I to tell Him to come?" So I tried, "Holy Spirit, please come," but that never sounded quite right. (I don't think He liked it either.) Finally I understood what it was all about. God so much wants to come; He loves to come; He is anxious to come; He wants this meeting to happen. But He is waiting for this word, this asking, to be spoken. Upon the invitation, "Come, Holy Spirit" the desire of His heart happens. He comes. The meeting, the *paga*, between Himself and the person begins.

Intercessory Teams and Ministry Teams Working Together

People usually refer to "intercessory teams" as groups who meet, often in private, to pray for situations some distance away. As we can see from the preceding discussion, intercession takes place in many other ministry situations as well. However, I will use "intercessory teams" in the way it is usually used, (which is not bad terminology since intercession is one of the major weapons this type of prayer team uses). I will use "ministry teams" to refer to teams who minister in the presence of the people for whom they pray. Both types of teams are invaluable. In the Body of Christ, different types of team prayer are like different modes of doing battle. Intercessory prayer teams go before the Lord asking Him to do things on behalf of others or on behalf of His cause. Their work is analogous to the air force or to special operations teams who infiltrate the front lines and aim their laser pointers at targets so that "smart bombs" can follow the beams and accurately destroy the enemy's fortresses. In intercessory team prayer, we aim our laser beams and say, "Okay God, over there." There may not be much power in the laser beams themselves, but when God comes in and bombs the specified targets we see His power break up the defenses.

[Note: We must pray Scripturally and in the way God desires it done. Before embarking on any spiritual warfare, I would recommend reading John Paul Jackson's *Needless*

Casualties of War. Francis Frangipanne's *The Three Battlegrounds* is also an excellent reference.]

If intercessory teams are like the air force, ministry teams are like the ground troops. The intercessory team prayer precedes the ground troops and softens the ground. Then ministry teams encounter the people and pray for them. Just as in military strategy, where the air force plays a critical role, intercessory prayer before ministry makes a tremendous difference. But the troops still must move in to take the land; teams in personal contact with the people are still needed. Some people are called to intercessory teams and others to ministry teams (and some to both). Both are vital. Some teams may not see visible signs of change when they pray— the final victory may be witnessed by another prayer team at a later time—nevertheless all have contributed to the final outcome. I often sense, when experiencing a victory, the years of intercession by someone like a loving grandmother that had made the difference.

Prophetic Prayer and Declaration

God sometimes has us declare His will in a prophetic prayer, word or declaration—to give voice to the command He is speaking. Often it is just before He is about to act. (Therefore, if you say something which God is not speaking, not very much is going to happen!) An example is found in Ezekiel 37:1. Ezekiel says, "The hand of the Lord was upon me, and He brought me out by the Spirit of the Lord and set me in the middle of a valley; it was full of bones. He led me back and forth among them, and I saw a great many bones on the floor of the valley, bones that were very dry. And he asked me, 'Son of man, can these bones live?' I said, 'Oh Sovereign Lord, You alone know.'" (That, by the way, is always a good answer! "You alone know." Ezekiel did not want to do his own will. He wanted to know, "What is God doing? What does He want? You tell me, God.")

The Lord tells him, "Prophesy to these bones and say to them, 'Dry bones, hear the word of the Lord! This is what the Sovereign Lord says to these bones: I will make breath enter you, and you will come to life. I will attach tendons to you and make flesh come upon you and cover you with skin; I will put breath in you, and you will come to life. Then you will know that I am the Lord.' So I prophesied as I was commanded. And as I was prophesying, there was a noise, a rattling sound, and the bones came together bone to bone."

In effect, the Lord told Ezekiel, "I want you to speak. Here's what I want you to say." As Ezekiel spoke these things, the Lord moved on behalf of His word. God knows what He wants to do, but there are times when He wants someone to speak it first.

When we are in a ministry situation praying for someone, we know that God could do whatever He wants done all by Himself. But one of the reasons we are there is to hear from the Lord and give voice to what He is saying. And, sometimes, even as the echo of those words is still in the air, He moves.

> **One of the reasons we are there is to hear from the Lord and give voice to what He is saying.**

Sometimes in a ministry situation you may not be sensing too much at first. Then someone speaks—a Scripture, a prophetic word, or a simple request of God—and suddenly you feel the presence of God rush in. They have just given expression to the heart of the Lord. When that happens the team needs to recognize what is happening and go with it. God might change direction later on, but right now stay with what He is doing. This is how to "go with the flow." When I feel the Spirit whoosh in, I ask myself, "What was just spoken? What was just prayed?" The increase of the Lord's presence might be a direct result of what just happened, giving us a sense of what the Father is doing.

Authority and the Heart of God

In talking about authority and the fact that our words count, let me stress again that this truth must always be understood in the context of our relationship with the Lord. We cannot just start saying words to make things happen. That is resorting to formulas, as discussed in Chapter Five. The words we speak have to be "what the Father is doing." We have to be in relationship—we have to have the heartbeat of the Lord.

In the movie *Braveheart*, in another of my favorite scenes, William Wallace's uncle came to take care of him right after his father's death. William stared in fascination at his uncle's gleaming Scottish sword. You know he was thinking, "Wow, that sword is cool!" But his uncle, reading his thoughts, cautioned him, "Before you learn to use this [pointing at the sword], you must learn to use this [pointing at his head]." Once, as I was watching the scene, I felt the Lord speaking to me, "Before you learn to use this [meaning any of the spiritual weapons He gives us], learn to use this [our heart]." That struck me deeply. It certainly applies to what we are talking about here.

While ministering at a meeting, a young woman was on the ministry team who, for a long time, had expressed a desire to hear from the Lord. She really wanted to hear His voice and be able to pray effectively for others. I had often said that the purest, and often the first, way to hear from the Lord is to feel His heart in our heart. As we began to pray for a person, I looked over at this girl and she was weeping. The Lord was actually allowing her to feel His heart, to feel the person's pain as He felt it Himself. She could do nothing but sit on the couch and cry the entire time we prayed.

When we prayed for a second person, the same thing happened; she sat on the couch and cried. The third was a homeless man. He sat in the center of the room while we prayed over him. Again, she was on the couch crying. But this time, she got up, came over, and asked him, "Were you ever beaten?" Before he could answer, she said, "I see a picture of you being beaten, and it was always around your head. The punches were always to your head. Is that true?"

He started crying and answered, "Yes."

She said, "It was your father, wasn't it?"

He just broke down and cried. He experienced a profound healing that night. When we led him into forgiving his father, we could almost physically see a burden lift off that young man and leave the room.

At the end of the meeting, someone drove him to where he was staying and asked, "How do you feel now?"

The young man said, "I feel lighter than I've ever felt in my life."

The driver asked, "Is that true about your father beating you?"

The young man said it was and added, "You know, the only place he ever struck me was on my face."

This young woman, who so desired to hear the Lord, had set the course of this ministry with that prophetic word. But before she had the word, she had felt the Father's heart.

The Kingdom of God

Our authority, our mission and who we are can be described in terms of the Kingdom of God. Jesus described His own ministry in these terms in Luke 4:43, one of more than one hundred references to "kingdom" in Matthew, Mark and Luke alone. The Kingdom of God is God's rule and reign in the hearts and minds of people. God's rule is a good one, characterized by truth, light, vitality, freedom and life. It is in contrast to the reign of the enemy, one of deceit, darkness, sickness, bondage and death. Jesus came as the point-man of a heavenly invasion, as it were, bringing in His Kingdom which obliterated that of the enemy wherever it went. When the Kingdom of God and the kingdom of the enemy met, it was often explosive (like the storm produced when warm moist air encounters a cold air mass). The works of the enemy were crushed. The dead came to life, the sick were healed, those in bondage set free.

As mentioned before, Jesus' death won back the keys Satan had taken, stripping his authority and winning for us pardon, life, right-standing, and authority. The victory was won. In military terms it was akin to D-Day, the point in World War II when historians agree that the outcome of the war was sealed. Yet some of the fiercest fighting was ahead as the allied troops took the land from a tyrannical foe. Jesus' second coming is akin to VE-Day (Victory in Europe Day), when the victory will be fully realized and we experience the Kingdom fully (unless we go to heaven first!). There He will wipe away every tear from our eye and sickness and death will reign no more. But for now, we live in an age when the Kingdom has come but not yet fully come—in the age when the Kingdom is both now and not yet. However, that Kingdom is breaking out wherever we go. Jesus preached the Kingdom with His words, but His works (miracles) demonstrated it was here through the crushing of the enemy's grip of deceit, death, disease, demons and destruction. (In Luke 10:9, for example, He sent the seventy-two to heal the sick and, in doing so, to proclaim, "The Kingdom of God has come near you.")

> **As we go, we, too, will see the Kingdom with its life and freedom burst on the scene, crushing the effects of the enemy's reign of destruction.**

Today He is sending us and as we go, we, too, will see the Kingdom with its life and freedom burst on the scene, crushing the effects of the enemy's reign of destruction. We don't know where or how it may burst out next, but it is its nature to do so. We, with Jesus at our side, are now point-men and women in the heavenly invasion, precipitators of God's Kingdom, as we bring His authority and very presence into a land that is ripe to be conquered. The part we play is often profoundly simple: a word of the Lord, an extension of our hand, or a deed of kindness, but it can precipitate an awesome work of the Lord as His Kingdom gloriously comes. Even small things, done with great love, can change the world. To encourage us to do these things, we need to know who we are and what we are about. We have the authority to ask and, therefore, experience, "Your Kingdom come, Your will be done on earth as it is in heaven." (For more background on the fascinating subject of the Kingdom of God, see George Eldon Ladd's *The Gospel of the Kingdom*.)

Royal Priests

It is written in 1 Peter 2:9 that, although we were once not a people, "[Now] you are a chosen people, a royal priesthood." The priest had the dual role of bringing God to the people and the people to God. He was the intercessor. The Lord is saying in 1 Peter that we are *each* called into this royal priesthood. Whether we realize it or not, He has made each of us to be priests. We are like ambassadors who go to another nation and ask the king to do something for that nation. And that king is incredibly eager to do what we ask.

It is hard to comprehend our position as priests and ambassadors, but when this truth does sink in, we also must realize and accept the responsibility that goes with it. We need to act accordingly. We are royal priests and God is listening to our words. He is telling us, "Go out, then, that I may pour out blessing on the people wherever you go. There are people living in darkness and you, My royal priests, need to go to them, raise your hands to heaven and ask that My mercy might fall on them."

Tips for Using Authority in Ministry

• **Seek relationship with God above all things.** Desire His heart to beat in yours. This is key to authority.

• **Realize God has given you power and authority.** Even though He knows what you are going to say or ask before you say it, saying it is part of exercising your authority.

• **Read the accounts of Elijah and other servants of God** and observe how they used authority. James says they were just like us (James 5:17).

• **Try incorporating petitional, prophetic and intercessory prayer in prayer ministry.** Ask, speak and welcome the meeting between the people and God's magnificent presence.

• **Try to sense the "flow" of the Spirit in ministry situations.** Look for an increased sense of His presence and ask yourself what was said or done (if anything) just before the increase happened. When that happens, stay in this flow and don't change directions for a while.

• **Contemplate about the Kingdom of God as it is used in the Lord's Prayer.** What was Jesus telling us to ask for in this prayer?

• **Realize you are a royal priest.** Ponder what you can release with your royal status.

Next time you look at yourself in the mirror, realize you are looking at a royal priest. It is imperative that we realize who we are in the Lord and the authority that He has given us— that He has chosen to partner with us. We need to go out into the world and be who and what we are.

To Dream the Possible Dream

Once as I was driving home, I started singing *To Dream the Impossible Dream*, a song that had regained some popularity at the time. As I was wailing, "To dream the impossible dream; to fight the unbeatable foe . . ." there was something in me that liked the idea that, even though it is impossible to win, I will go out there and fight anyway. As I was singing, I felt the Lord say, "What are you singing about? Fight the unbeatable foe?" As I pondered that, He said, "What makes you think the foe is unbeatable? He's not unbeatable." And then He added, "Where you go, there are going to be battles that are overwhelmingly won by Me. And you already know that, at the end of the Book, I am the winner." (This is not to deny an end-time battle so terrible that only God's intervention can save us, but that is no excuse not to fight while it is still day.)

I admit that it is easy to sink into a defeatist attitude. We have cities where crime, drugs and gangs are a terrible plague, and we conceive of the church as a haven for people to escape these things. It is hard to imagine the church could be used to significantly change or eradicate these evils. But the Lord says, "Get rid of that attitude!"

When Jesus talked to Peter in Matthew 16:18, He said, "I will build my church and the gates of hell will not overcome it." In reading this verse, we often picture the enemy prowling around with the church over in a corner, being told, "Don't worry, you won't get beaten up to the point of being overcome. The gates of hell won't overcome you." But that is not what this passage is saying. Gates don't prowl around. Gates are not an offensive weapon. Have you ever been chased by a gate? This verse is saying that the gates will not prevail when we attack *them*. It is saying that when you go out into the world asking the Kingdom of Heaven to come and you encounter the enemy's gates, they will not be able to withstand *you*! You will prevail. Those gates are there to protect the enemy and maintain all he has captured. God says they will not be able to resist our attack; these gates will fly open. And all who are bound are going to be free! The dream is possible; the foe is beatable! The Kingdom of God *will* come; no gates are strong enough to stand in its way. It was true of Jesus. It is true of us, His church.

> **We are like Elijah and the prophets of old, who were told to speak and ask as precursors to the move of the Lord.**

We are like Elijah and the prophets of old, who were told to speak and ask as precursors to the move of the Lord. At Mt. Carmel, in the face of seemingly overwhelming odds, Elijah did not hesitate to shut the gates of the enemy's power and open the gates of God's (I Kings 18:16-46). He asked and received a demonstration of God's reality and power, toppling the enemy's gates and giving his people a hope in God whose arm was not too short to save them. Our God is that God—the same yesterday, today and forever. We can be that Elijah if we realize who we are, seek to be in relationship with Him and, as His Spirit moves with power, speak what He is saying and do what He is doing. He has given us authority. He has made us royal priests. It's beyond a dream to dream: it's a life to live.

8

The Prophetic Ministry: Hearing from God

You may have noticed in previous chapters how often I spoke about hearing from God. Listening is part of our relationship with the Holy Spirit. Our approach to healing is based upon discerning what the Father is doing. Imparting hope may involve speaking a prophetic word. Authority is often the result of hearing what God is saying and verbalizing it. Now I would like to focus on hearing God's voice as a subject by itself and present some helps for hearing His voice more clearly.

Telling people that you talk to God can raise a few eyebrows. Telling them that God answers you back may make them doubt your sanity! Unfortunately, even in the church, the idea that God speaks directly to us is often not considered normative Christianity. However, Scripture, not the experience or opinion of man, must tell us what is normal. Cover to cover, Scripture contains over 2100 verses showing God speaking to people. Christianity is about a relationship between God and man initiated by a desire so strong the Father gave His one and only Son. As in any relationship, communication is important. Can you imagine a relationship without it? Or a relationship where one partner did all the talking and the other only listened? Neither partner would like that.

When I say "hearing from God" in this chapter, I am not just referring to hearing words; God can speak to us in a number of ways (which I will enumerate later). The Bible itself is the main means of hearing from God. It is His clear and undisputed voice and our sole source of doctrine. However, we often need specific direction for specific situations, especially when we want to do His will in ministry settings. The Bible was not written to be a list of specific instructions for every circumstance we might ever encounter. (That's probably not even possible and, even if it were, in the natural realm we often don't know what all the circumstances are.) The Bible does give us general instructions, yet it also portrays God as One who will speak to us about specific details in our life and show us the way. Looking at His relationship with Moses and David, for example, we can see that He loves His people close to Him, praying, asking, talking and listening to His voice. He wants us to draw close.

Earnestly Desire to Prophesy

In 1 Corinthians 12-14 Paul discusses spiritual gifts. Many of these gifts involve hearing from God. That is, they are *prophetic* in nature. Some say that we are now in the New Testament age and no longer in the age of the prophets; prophecy is therefore a thing of the past. But Paul is talking about gifts for the New Testament age. There were, in fact, prophets in this age (although, in one respect, they had a different role than Old Testament prophets—this I will discuss in detail in Chapter Ten). In fact, I would argue prophecy is to be more prevalent in this age than ever before. Our age is the answer to the cry of Moses, "I wish that all the Lord's people were prophets" (Numbers 11:29). The age in which we now live—now that Pentecost has come—is a fulfillment of Joel 2:28 as quoted in Acts 2:17-18, "In the last days I will pour out My Spirit on all people. Your sons and daughters will prophesy, your young men will see visions, your old men will dream dreams. Even on My servants, both men and women,

I will pour out My Spirit in those days, and they will prophesy."

In the opening verses of 1 Corinthians 12-14, Paul uses the term "dumb idols." The word "dumb" means, "cannot talk." He is contrasting this with God who *can and does* speak! He then says, "No one can say 'Jesus is Lord' except by the Spirit." The experience, common to every Christian, of something inside us telling us Jesus is Lord, is actually the supernatural experience of hearing His voice. It is the same dynamic which is behind the prophetic gifts, which Paul discusses in the following verses.

In 1 Corinthians 14:1 Paul exhorts us to, literally in the Greek, "earnestly desire to prophesy." The Greek for "earnestly desire" is a strong word, the same word that is translated "covet" in other places. Paul says this once again at the end of 1 Corinthians 14, showing how heartfelt his yearning is that we have a desire to hear from God.

Prophecy in the Old and New Testaments

The verb "prophesy" refers to receiving and giving information supernaturally obtained from God. Its use in Scripture shows that it has a supernatural element—the information received was not naturally known to the person doing the prophesying. (See, for example, John 4:17-19 and Luke 7:39.) It was revealed by God.

People often think of prophecy as a prediction of the future. But in the Old Testament, prediction was only part of it. The Old Testament prophets also spoke forth, to the nations or to the people of God, what was on God's heart. Therefore prophecy was either "fore-telling" or "forth-telling."

The "fore-telling" aspect was important because it gave a "stamp" to the actions God was about to do. Whenever the prophets said that God was about to do something and then He did it, everyone knew that it was God who did it; it was not some sort of random happenstance. The "forth-telling" told people what was on God's heart. Sometimes it was an authoritative speaking forth as described in the previous chapter—as they spoke, God acted.

Old Testament prophecy was expressed not only in words but sometimes in actions. For example, the "action prophecy" of smashing a clay pot was laden with meaning— a forewarning of the destruction of Jerusalem. Even in the New Testament, baptism and communion have an "action-prophetic" element—the actions of dipping, breaking, eating and drinking carry meaning and are as much an expression of His voice as a spoken or written word. In ministry, sometimes God may have us say something to express His will; sometimes He may have us do something.

In the New Testament Paul lays out purposes of the prophetic gifts and ministry in several places. In 1 Corinthians 14:3 Paul says prophecy is for "strengthening, encouragement and comfort." A prophetic word can speak to our *present* situation, giving us strength (or edification), to our *past*, giving us comfort, or to our *future*, encouraging us to go forth.

In 1 Corinthians 14:22-25 Paul says that prophesying can cause unbelievers to come to God, causing them to "fall down and worship God, exclaiming 'God is really among you!'" In other words, prophecy has a powerful role to play in evangelism. (More on this later!)

In 1 Timothy 1:18 and 4:14 Paul refers to another purpose for prophecy: to give direction and impart gifts to a person's life and ministry. Often, throughout the Book of Acts, we see revelation playing an important role in directing people and ministries. (See, for example, Acts 8:26-29, Acts 10:9-33 and Acts 16:6-10).

Prophecy in the Early Church

History records that God did not stop speaking to His people at the end of the Book of Acts—He continued speaking with the Early Church and beyond that, into our day. One early church father, Irenaeus (130-200 AD), was indignant as he wrote about a group called the Alogi who claimed that prophecy had ceased (*Proof of Apostolic Preaching* 99). Justin Martyr (100-165), Origen (185-254) and Gregory of Nyssa (335-395) all pointed to the prophetic activity and miracles of their day as signs that testified to the world the veracity of the Christian faith (*Dialog with Trypho* 82, *Against Celsus* 2.8, *Commentary on Song of Songs* 6). Epiphanius (347-407), a church historian, wrote of the prophetic gift, "But the gift is not inoperative in the holy Church, far from it!" (*Panarion* 48.1). Many martyrs (for example, Polycarp in 156, John Huss in 1415, George Wishat in 1546) spoke remarkable prophetic words near the times of their martyrdom. In recent church history, prophetic revelation has been given to many of the people who fathered our current mainline denominations. Jack Deere, in his book *Surprised by the Voice of God*, devotes a chapter to prophetic activity among the fathers of the Presbyterian movement.

Logos and Rhema

An interesting word study, which helps explain the usefulness of the prophetic gifts, especially in the context of team ministry, is the comparison of the two Greek words for "word," *logos* and *rhema*. In the Bible, logos usually pertains to the entirety of the revealed Word. In John 1, for example, Jesus was called the Logos—everything God was and stood for was embodied in Jesus. Rhema, when translated word, usually refers to a specific word. When ministering to a person, time considerations make it difficult to give the person the logos—that is, to read him the entire Bible!

However, God may have a specific word, or rhema, which is the perfect word for this particular time and situation. In the section of Ephesians 6 which describes the full armor of God, Paul talks about "the sword of the Spirit, which is the word of God" (Eph. 6:17). Here the word for "word" is rhema. The sword referred to was a short sword with a round, narrow blade. It was designed to be thrust through a chink in the opponent's armor. In the same way, when a person, because of hurt in the past, has placed thick barriers over his heart, the rhema word, a prophetic word given by God, can find its way past those defenses and penetrate into his heart. I have seen this happen many times; the person becomes undone, his defenses fall away, and the truth of God's good news can enter his heart and do its work.

The Three Elements of Prophesying

The gift or ministry of prophecy is actually more than just hearing God's voice. It involves three elements: revelation (hearing God's voice), interpretation (interpreting what we hear), and application (deciding how, when and if we should say what we have heard). All three are important and each requires hearing from God. For example, in ministering I might supernaturally hear the word "abuse" (the revelation). Before I would say anything, however, I need the correct interpretation: was the person abused, was he or she an abuser, what kind of abuse was involved? I would ask God for His answer and wait for more information. (Sometimes I might simply ask the person.) After feeling I have the correct interpretation, I still need the application: how do I say this word? Again I would ask God. Perhaps I would be led to not say anything at this time—just pray about it or perhaps, if I were praying for a woman, I might ask another woman to talk with her in another setting. If I feel that now is the time to speak, I would first ask God for His heart that I might speak as He would speak. How we say a word can have as much (or more) impact than what we say. Without the heart of God, it is best not to say anything.

Testing What We Hear

1 Corinthians 14:29 says, "Two or three prophets should speak, and the others should weigh carefully what is said." Of course, the first person that should test a revelation is the person who receives it—before he gives it! The fact is, we all "prophesy in part" (1 Corinthians 13:9) and sometimes we get it right and sometimes we do not (and sometimes only partially right). We—and the church—need to know this so we and they can weigh what is said. Notice that Paul accepts the fact that some prophetic words are hits and others misses and, unless a person's heart was not right (which he addresses in chapter 13), he does not come down harshly on those speaking—he just warns those hearing to weigh what is said. (In Chapter Ten I will address Deuteronomy 18:20 which refers to prophecy in a different context and level and gives a death penalty for prophesying something false.)

As we ourselves move in the prophetic gifts, we must avoid falling into the trap of thinking that our prophetic ministry is nearly infallible and that for someone to doubt or test our words is tantamount to doubting God Himself. This lack of humility gets us into trouble. The main person we fool when we fall into this trap is ourselves. I once heard a well-known individual who moves with a remarkable prophetic anointing estimate that his accuracy rate was a certain percent—a figure I thought very modest considering the amazing accuracy and detail of the words he gave to people I knew. He said that he was praying it would get higher. If he could have the humility to say that, how much more so we. But even if the accuracy were as high as 95% or even 99%, it would still be wrong once in a while, meaning that we (and others) still have to test the prophetic words. So how do we test them?

We (and others) have to test the prophetic words.

The first test for prophetic words is to weigh them against Scripture. They must not contradict Scripture nor add anything doctrinal that is not in Scripture. They must also agree with the *spirit* of Scripture. For example, we must ask ourselves, could we picture Jesus saying those words, or would they be out of character with who He is?

Second, we must look at the fruit of the prophetic word. If it is a word from God, it will not return void but will accomplish what He desires (Isaiah 55:11); it will bear fruit.

Third, we must look at the fruit of the prophet. What is his or her track record for accuracy? What fruit of the Spirit have they sown? We realize that no one hits 100%, but is the person humble, correctable and teachable? Try to separate fruit from appearances. Some may put on "prophetic airs," with little fruit but lots of "fruitiness" (they think their weirdness somehow validates them). On the other hand, the operation of a true gift (or the presence of the Lord) may sometimes appear strange and offend your mind. (God sometimes purposely offends our minds to reveal to ourselves our hearts.) Judge by fruit, not methods. If we judged by methods, what would we do with Isaiah who walked around naked for three years, or Ezekiel who baked his bread over a fire of burning cow manure? Some of the prophets in the Bible were very unusual while others were very ordinary human beings. The point is, you cannot judge by methods and outward appearances; you must judge by fruit. To those I train, however, I say, please don't *try* to be unusual or put on airs; be natural; be yourselves.

Fourth, look for a witness in yourself and others. As a person is giving a prophetic word, God may also be speaking to you or others about the truth and applicability of that word. God gives the gift of discernment to His church. Sometimes discernment is experienced simply as a "sense" that this word is from God; sometimes it comes in the form of wisdom, perhaps in knowing how to test it.

Fifth, ask those to whom the word is given if it is true, if it makes sense to them, what their thoughts are about it. Discern the accuracy of the word and if it brought them closer to God. Although, it may be impossible to do this with each and every prophetic word you give, try to get as much feedback as possible. This not only benefits you, helping you grow in accuracy by learning from your hits and misses, but it also benefits them, clarifying what was said, rectifying what was incorrect, correcting what they mistakenly thought you meant, and giving opportunity for further ministry. Sometimes the word may be true, but the person may not be in tune with what you said or may not admit that it was true. However, we must have a humble attitude and realize that we only prophesy in part—give the person the benefit of the doubt. If it was true and they did not acknowledge it, it is their problem. We have done our part and must let it go. If we go around prophesying without knowing or caring whether the words we said were true and without getting validation by the recipients, it's like playing a game of basketball in a court without hoops. We don't really know how many hits or misses we make and we don't get any better at the game. It can even lead us to think that all our human-induced hunches and mistaken impressions are "words from the Lord." Our own unvalidated "prophetic" thoughts can then influence our thinking either positively or negatively—producing feelings for people that aren't reality-based. (I call this "prophetic prejudice"—we are prejudiced by our own negative feelings which we mislabel as prophetic insight. Like any kind of prejudice, this is bad and not from the Lord!)

Finally, realize that if several different prophetic words were given in a ministry situation (for instance, one saying they need healing, another encouraging them about their future, a third affirming a gift of the Holy Spirit), it does not necessarily mean that only one word is true and the others are not. God may want to minister all of these in the course of the ministry session. You must discern which the Lord wants to do first.

The Risk and Worth of Prophecy

When I teach this material in a training session, I like to give opportunity to *do* it, not just learn about it. Often I pick a willing volunteer to receive ministry from the entire group. After a time of waiting on the Lord, the group will share with the person the words, visions and impressions the Lord has given them. Their prophetic words often dovetail and confirm one another. The unusual word which someone is hesitant to say is often the most meaningful and profound. I have observed that it can take a lot of courage to speak a prophetic word for the first time. In reality, speaking these words will *always* take courage, although you will eventually get used to it and may even start to like the thrill!

If it takes courage to give words in a ministry session inside your church or home, it takes even more courage to give them out in the world! Realizing the evangelistic aspect of the prophetic gifts, Jon, a friend from the early days I spoke of in Chapter One, earnestly desired to be used in evangelistic prophecy. When he first began, I did not notice that he had any latent prophetic gift, although I have rarely seen anyone with so much desire for one! (He eventually became quite gifted and discipled a couple who now have a recognized prophetic ministry.)

In the early days, as Jon was gaining experience in the use of the prophetic gifts, he happened to be standing in line at an ice cream shop when he felt that he had a word for the woman serving him ice cream. He felt that perhaps her father was in the hospital and God wanted to say something about it. Finally he mustered up enough courage to ask her, "Is your father in the hospital?"

She was a little taken aback and said, "Not that I know of! Is he? Is he all right?"

Embarrassed, Jon tried to assure her that he was probably ok. He tried to think of an excuse for his strange behavior, perhaps telling her it was the food he ate, but he hadn't gotten his order yet, so he couldn't blame it on that! Later he asked the Lord, "What was that? I thought I heard You!"

The Lord spoke to him, "You missed it, but I'm proud of you for trying. You're in boot camp. Keep at it."

A few days later Jon was driving down the road and saw a group of teenagers congregated at a park bench. Jon thought he heard the Lord say, "They're talking about suicide."

Thinking, "Oh, no, not again!" Jon decided, "What have I got to lose?" So he parked his car, walked up to the young men and said, "You're going to think this is weird, but sometimes the Lord speaks to me. I was driving down the road and, when I saw you, I thought I heard the Lord say you were talking about suicide."

Their jaws just about dropped to the ground. That is exactly what they were talking about! This gave Jon the entrance to talk to them about the Lord. He had their complete attention.

A while after that, he saw a man in a courthouse with long, greased-back hair and felt the Lord wanted him to ask the man if he ever went to a particular conservative Baptist college. Jon asked him (even though the man did not look conservative or Baptist!), mentioning the college by name. The man, surprised, asked, "How did you know that?" This gave Jon the courage to ask if he could pray for him. As soon as they began to pray, the man began to weep under the power of the Holy Spirit. Jon asked him about his marriage and the man began to weep even harder. That was a pivotal moment in that man's life. God healed his marriage and launched him and his wife into a marriage ministry of their own.

Let me say that taking risks is normally not this extreme! The truth is, if we take what we think is a huge risk and we miss it, the consequence is usually not as adverse as we think it will be. In fact, people usually just end up realizing that we care. They also realize that we have enough faith in the reality of God to take a risk.

Like Jon's encounter with the man at the courthouse, taking risks can bring enormous dividends. In Jack Deere's *Surprised by the Voice of God*, Jack gives an example of a prophetic word and the benefit it bestowed to the hearer. (Taken from *Surprised by the Voice of God* by Jack S. Deere, pp. 65-66. Copyright ©1996 by Jack S. Deere. Used by permission of The Zondervan Corporation.)

> I looked over at the prophetically gifted pastor I had brought in with me and said, "Has the Lord shown you anything about these kids? He sure isn't showing me much."
>
> "Yes he has," he said. "He has shown me something about this young lady right here," with that he pointed to a young, cute twelve-year-old girl sitting in the front row, "about that young man back there," he pointed to a twelve-year-old boy sitting in the middle of the room, "and about this lady in the back," he pointed to one of the Sunday school teachers in the back of the room.
>
> He looked at the young girl. "What's your name?" he asked.
>
> "J-J-Julie." Julie was not so sure she wanted someone giving her a prophetic word in front of two hundred of her peers.
>
> "Julie, while Jack was speaking I had a vision of you. It was Tuesday night. That's five nights ago. You went to your bedroom and shut the door. You were crying. You looked up to heaven and said, 'God, do you really love me? I have to know—do you really love me?' God didn't say anything to you

on Tuesday night, Julie. He sent me here tonight to tell you he really loves you. He really loves you. He also told me to tell you that the trouble going on around you is not your fault. He didn't tell me if he is going to change the trouble, but he wants you to know you aren't the cause of it."

Then he went on to say something about the young man and something about the lady. After it was all over, I called those three people up to the front so we could talk privately. I wanted to make sure of two things: one, that there were no misunderstandings between the people and the prophetic minister, and two, that everything that had been said was true. If part of the messages given to these people was false, then we wanted to own up to it and clear up any misconceptions.

"Julie, last Tuesday night were you in your bedroom crying really hard, and did you ask God if he really loved you?" I asked.

"Yes."

"Are your parents fighting now?"

"Yes."

"Are they talking about getting a divorce?"

"Yes."

"Do you think that's your fault?"

She looked up at me, smiled, and said, "Not any more."

I walked out of church that night thinking, *Who in the world could be against this ministry? Why wouldn't anyone want the voice of the Lord to speak like this in their church?* . . . Then I thought about a little twelve-year-old girl in Anaheim, California, who won't be sitting in some psychiatrist's office when she is thirty years old, trying to get rid of guilt she has carried around for the last twenty years.

Ways God Can Speak to Us

Someone once did a study in Scripture of all the different ways God has spoken to people. The list became so long that he finally concluded that God speaks to people in every conceivable way! As Hebrews 1:1 states, God has spoken "at many times and in various ways." Interestingly, some of the more unusual ways, mentioned at the end of my list, are more frequent in Scripture than the ways we would consider more common. Here are some of the ways God speaks to us.

First, the Lord might "pop" words into our minds. He might give a phrase, several sentences, or a Scripture verse. Sometimes a single word might come into someone's mind. I remember times when this happened and we did not know what the word meant. Going to the dictionary, we looked it up, read the definition out loud and found it to be an exact fit for the situation!

Similarly, pictures can "pop" into our minds. God tends to speak in a way that suits each of us personally. Some people are more visually oriented and others are more verbal. The picture may be literal or symbolic. Some symbolism is universal. Clear, moving water, for example, almost always represents the Holy Spirit, while other symbols may be part of the "language" the Lord develops uniquely between Himself and you.

Sometimes we just "know" what God is saying. I call that "popping a pattern" into our mind. This is often how it works with me. All of a sudden I get an understanding about something or someone, and I start exploring the "pattern" He has put in my mind, getting more details or specific words from the Lord along the way.

Sometimes God will give us a few words to say and we start speaking. After giving those words, a few more come, and then a few more. This can feel scary, but sometimes that is the way it happens.

Sometimes He speaks through physical sensations. For example in Luke 8:46, Jesus perceived a flow of power from Him as a woman touched the hem of His garment for healing. As mentioned in Chapter Three, when praying for physical healing, physical sensations can help discern what the Father is doing. Sometimes the Lord allows us to feel the same pain as others (sympathetic pains), either as a prophetic "word of knowledge" to identify people with this malady and invite them to come forward for prayer, or simply to give us compassion for them and allow us to know how they feel. Sometimes what I feel within myself helps me know where or what to pray for another.

> ## Often God lets us know His will by letting us feel His heart.

Often God lets us know His will by letting us feel His heart. I have found that the experience of feeling what God has put into our heart is an excellent way to begin learning how to prophesy. It establishes the importance of communicating prophetic words with His heart, one of the most important ingredients in giving a prophetic word.

God can also speak through visions and dreams. Visions vary from what seem like "dreams while we are awake" to "really being there." Sometimes people see a spiritual reality superimposed over what is seen in the physical realm. Visions are usually literal, whereas dreams are often symbolic.

Scripture also talks about being "caught up in the Spirit," angelic visitations, hearing the audible voice of God, and many other unusual means of communication. Every one of these ways which God speaks to people has been recorded in Scripture, throughout the history of the church, and in our day, with accounts from people in virtually every denomination.

Hints for Ministering Prophetically

In the early days, I was fascinated with the prophetic gifts and said to myself that if I ever learned how to use them, I would teach others. When I finally did start moving in them, I realized that I did not know how I was doing it! God was good enough to speak to me and He knew how to get through my thick head! As true as that was, along the way I still picked up some helps that are useful for moving in the prophetic gifts. Actually, they are appropriate for moving in any of the gifts of the Spirit.

• Keep your eyes on Jesus and your relationship with Him. Ask for His presence and His heart for the person.

• Move in God's presence and His peace. If you start losing that, just stop and turn to get back into His presence again. Worship, pray in the Spirit, read His word, or do whatever brings you into His presence. As mentioned earlier, you don't have to "work yourself up." Don't put yourself under that kind of pressure.

• If you feel an unction from the Lord—a feeling to do or say something—move on it. Sometimes His directions are there one second and gone the next, and, if you toy with them too long, you will lose them. By "move on it" I mean that you might say it right then, later in private, later in intercession, or you might just "put it on file" for future reference.

• Remember that in prophetic ministry, three things must happen accurately: revelation, interpretation, and application. Getting the right interpretation and application are as much a part of the prophetic process as getting the revelation itself. If you get a revelation, go to the Lord and ask Him what it means and how and when to say it. You are constantly dependent on the Lord for all three.

In prophetic ministry, three things must happen accurately: revelation, interpretation, and application.

• A friend of ours notes that in prayer ministry, we can get impatient when nothing happens and there can be a temptation to fill in the gaps with our own words. However, with practice, a sense comes and a word from ourselves just doesn't feel or even sound right. If this happens, back up and ask the Lord for help before continuing on. Also, be comfortable with silence (the Lord may be doing something else at this time) and don't pressure yourself to fill in any gaps. Another friend told of a dream in which the Lord handed out tests to a room full of students. Everyone was writing furiously, while my friend handed in a blank page. After the papers were graded, he got an A. The Lord said the test was to see if you would write anything down before He started speaking! My experience has been that often He speaks right away, and almost always He will speak eventually, but sometimes the test is to wait.

• Sometimes you may receive words that you are not too confident about. Pray about speaking them (and whether the timing is right), but realize that words that sound nonsensical to you might have a great deal of meaning to the hearer. Sometimes you just have to try. Sometimes what you receive from the Lord may sound too mundane, but I have repeatedly seen simple things touch someone profoundly—a simple prayer or just saying "God loves you."

• Be honest and open. Admit and learn from your success and failures. If other people give words that you feel are from the Lord, confirm them. That's how we all learn to prophesy better. We can be a help and encouragement to each other.

• In your quiet times alone with the Lord, sometimes writing down the words from Him helps. It can clear your mind to receive more. You can also refer to them for future reference.

• Earnestly desire to prophesy, as Paul admonished us in 1 Corinthians 14:1 and 39. Have faith—God will certainly give the Holy Spirit to those who ask (Luke 11:13). Our God is a God who speaks—at many times and in various ways. Ask Him to teach you to hear and be open to the different ways He may speak.

Earnestly desire to prophesy.

• Take risks. It really helps to grow in the spiritual gifts in an atmosphere that is conducive to risk taking. For that reason small groups—where you create a shared understanding that it is a safe place to try out words and make mistakes—are an ideal place for people to grow in the prophetic gifts. Safe practice can give you confidence to use your gifts in "riskier" situations.

• Ask yourself, "What would God say if He were here?" Once I was with a small group of college students. We weren't even talking about prophecy, but during ministry time I said, "If God were here, what would He want to say to each of you? Just pray and look around the room and tell each other what you think He would say to them if He were here." They thought for a while and prayed. Then one girl looked up and said to another, "Well, you know, if God were here, I think He would tell you . . ." and started saying it. When she spoke, we could feel the Holy Spirit resonate with her words. Then another person spoke, "If God were here, I think He would say . . ." and again we could feel the Spirit on his words. Finally I realized, this is prophecy! These are God's words to these people! Then I realized that when I said,

"What would God say to us *if He were here*?" that He *was* here—and always is, where two or three are gathered in His name—and He was speaking!

• Probably the most important help for moving in the prophetic (or any of the gifts) is to be intimate with God. The closer you get to Him, the closer you feel His heart and the more you will know His will. Our hearts must beat as one with His; it is absolutely necessary. Find every way you can to know Him better: read His Word, spend time with Him, fellowship with others who love Him. Always ask for His presence to be with you and upon you, both in quiet times and when you minister.

• Believe that God will speak and is able to make you hear Him. It is really not all that complicated. I think people can hear from God a lot more easily than they think. In fact, I think a lot of times God speaks to people and they don't even realize it. If we can learn to recognize when and how He speaks, we can be much more open to hearing from Him, willing to take risks, and will listen attentively more often.

Keep Trying!

My encouragement is: Keep trying! I love when people who think that they could never hear God's voice hear Him. A few years ago this happened to a friend of mine. He said he could never picture himself hearing God. Then things began to change. His first experience was a dream. He dreamed he was in a battlefield and reached down and picked up a pole which turned out to be a banner that was almost unrecognizable because it was covered in mud. He realized that this banner symbolized what his life was about. Then it started to rain. And as it rained, the mud started washing off the banner. He could almost see what it said, but then he woke up. He knew this was about his life; he had recently come to the Lord and was transitioning from a life muddied by the effects of alcoholism and mistakes he had made to a life renewed by God. But he still could not see what his life was about.

Some months later he had another dream. Again he had a banner in his hand and now it was clean. He had run up on a hill and was planting the banner on top of it. As he woke up, eight Scripture references came to his mind which he wrote down. Each was the name of a book and the number of a verse—he had no idea what the text of each verse was. In fact, being a new Christian, he had so little prowess of Scripture that he did not even know where to find those books in the Bible except by using the table of contents! That morning he told his wife about the dream and then afterwards suddenly remembered the Scripture references he had jotted down. The two of them looked them up. Each one referred to banners! (I didn't even know there were that many verses in the Bible about banners!) He was amazed at the dream, even more amazed at the Scripture references, but exceedingly amazed at the fact that God would speak to him. God can speak to us all. Ask Him.

Towards Purer Revelation

Once you start moving in the prophetic, it is important to start moving toward purer revelation. Here are some things that will help in that process. (Again, what I am telling you here could be applied to any gift.)

First and foremost, keep growing in intimacy with Him. Some of my best times were alone with Him where I would ask Him to pray for me, as I would a prayer team, and then just receive all He wanted to do. (This is not to say I would do this in lieu of receiving ministry from prayer teams—far from it! Fellowship with and ministry from others is vital. But so is our time alone with God.)

Next, grow in holiness and purity. Sinful attitudes such as selfish ambition, a desire to control others, resistance to being corrected, bitterness, rejection, or insecurity can lead to mistakes in what we think we are hearing from the Lord. They are like a loud radio that is blaring in our spirit. As we hear something from the Lord, things from this "radio" can get mixed in. The more sanctified you become, the less interference will be coming from this radio, and the purer you will be in the prophetic gifts.

Practice and grow in hearing His voice often. Learn from your "hits" and "misses"—you learn from experience what His voice is like and what it is not. It's like getting a telephone call; when people have called often enough, you can tell who it is as soon as they say hello, before they even tell you their name.

Have a willingness to wait—for God to speak, for permission to say what He spoke, or to ask if God has anything more to say. Those who have grown in the prophetic ministry have also grown in this willingness to wait.

One of the major ways to grow in the prophetic ministry is having a good understanding of law and grace. This is such a major topic, however, that I have devoted an entire chapter to it. That is next.

9

The Power of the Law; the Power of Grace

As ministry team members mature, they usually grow in hearing from the Lord, flowing with the Spirit's power and every other aspect of the ministry. But one area that is often a sticking point in their forward progress is the effective use of law and grace. On the surface, law and grace are simple to understand. However, our upbringing, education and life experiences can cast a shadow over the way we view and use them, ultimately affecting the way we minister to others. That is why I am devoting a chapter to this subject. It is a fitting topic to follow the discussion of prophetic ministry because it will lead to many applications for ministering prophetically.

Both law and grace have their own power and it is imperative to understand how each works and to not use one when the other is called for. Martin Luther had a deep understanding of this. His grasp of it was so great that scholars agree that his writings on law and grace were cutting edge both in his day and today. To pursue the Second Reformation, we must learn from the first one.

An example of how *not* to use the law will lead us to understand and appreciate how to use both the law and grace.

Legalism

Legalism is the most common misuse of the law. It was the major flaw in the Pharisee's way of thinking. A surprisingly large number of New Testament verses are devoted to the Pharisees. They are mentioned by name almost one hundred times. Curious, isn't it? On a time scale, the era in which the Pharisees actually existed was very short, about 200 years, in comparison to the large span of time covered in the Bible. Why is so much attention given to them? I think it is because it's so easy for *us* to fall into the very same way of thinking. Jesus, in fact, warned us of this in Matthew 16:6: "Beware of the leaven of the Pharisees."

Like leaven, legalism starts as a little thing that penetrates our souls. It keeps growing and growing and, before we know it, affects our entire life. Its danger is in how unaware we can be that it is within us. We must never allow ourselves to think that we don't have any of the Pharisee's leaven in us, because we all do. None of us are free from it. We have to be able to identify it so we can ask the Lord to help us deal with it.

Even though we know that we have been saved by grace, we can still easily slip into legalism. In Galatians 3:1-5 Paul said, "You foolish Galatians, are you so foolish, after beginning with the spirit, are you now trying to attain perfection by human efforts?" Legalism has always been an easy trap to fall into.

To explain what legalism is, let me first paint a picture that many people—both inside and outside the church—have (at least in part) about Christianity. In this picture, as people enter the church, they see hoops set up before them. People are jumping through these hoops, some with great dexterity, some barely making them at all. Most of the hoops are good things like praying, reading the Bible, going to meetings and getting to church on time. Some of the hoops are lower— everyone is expected to jump through them—but some hoops are very high and people watch as "super-Christians," seemingly without effort, skillfully jump through. Many watching get downhearted because they can barely jump through the lower hoops, let alone the higher ones; the high ones seem impossible—so unattainable it is hopeless.

To many, this is what Christianity is about: trying to jump through hoops. Of course, there is nothing wrong with prayer, reading the Bible, getting to church on time and so forth. We've got to pray, and reading the Bible is essential. The problem comes in the way we view these activities—and how we view Christianity in general.

Using this picture we can illustrate what legalism is and recognize the conditions it needs to grow. Legalism occurs when one of two things happen: first, when we think we can earn God's favor by jumping through these hoops (or lose His favor when we miss) or second, when we fail to recognize that there is no power in the hoops themselves that can help us jump through them. Saying this another way, legalism occurs when we think we can earn God's favor by what we do (or lose His favor by what we fail at doing) or when we think that telling people what to do empowers them to do it. These two errors may seem like minor inaccuracies in the way we think Christianity works, but they have major consequences in our lives and in the life of the church.

Falling into legalism usually results in despair or hypocrisy. You may despair: you simply cannot make it through the hoops. You feel frustrated and condemned. Or you may swing the other way, towards hypocrisy. If you can successfully jump through some of the hoops, you may feel quite pleased with yourself, fooling yourself into thinking you have it made and are definitely special. That is the route the Pharisees took. If you travel far enough down the Pharisaical road, you will eventually wind up standing in opposition to God by constructing a religion that involves jumping through hoops. Such a religion stands against the true Kingdom of God and can keep people from accessing God or attaining real spiritual growth.

When you fall into legalism, it's easy to start putting up hoops for others to jump through and then criticize them when they fail. This can happen even if you fall into legalism with no malicious intent, perhaps because you were brought up that way or because you developed a hard, rigid view of God from being treated harshly. You unknowingly try to put legalistic constrictions upon those to whom you talk or minister.

In Scriptural terminology, the "law" is what I have described as "hoops." The law tells us what we are supposed to do (or avoid doing). Defining legalism in terms of the law, legalism occurs when we think we can earn God's approval through the law or when we fail to recognize that the law has no power in itself to help us fulfill it. Legalism occurs when we try to use the law for something only grace can do.

> **Legalism occurs when we think we can earn God's approval through the law or when we fail to recognize that the law has no power in itself to help us fulfill it.**

God's approval does not come from what we do. It is a gift—grace—received by faith. And it is only by grace that we are empowered to do good. Our own works, our own jumping through hoops, do not empower us. Legalistic hoop jumping and works that are inspired by grace may look the same, but they are very different at the heart. If you need Scriptural backing for any of this, Paul talks extensively about these very things in Romans 1-7, Galatians 1-5 and Ephesians 1-2.

The law is good and has a power of its own, but it never helps us jump through hoops or gain God's approval. Only grace does that. Two stories in the Gospels, the rich young ruler and Zacchaeus, illustrate this perfectly and launch us towards the right use of the law and grace.

The Rich Young Ruler

In Mark 10 (as well as in Luke 18), three stories follow each other: Jesus blessing the children, Jesus challenging the rich young ruler and Jesus predicting his death on the way to Jerusalem. Sometimes insights can be gained by looking at the connections between a passage and the surrounding verses. So, to look at the account of the rich young ruler, let us begin with the first of these three stories.

As the chapter begins, Jesus is teaching the people when the Pharisees begin questioning him about divorce. Then people bring little children to Jesus for His blessing. The disciples, assuming Jesus does not want to be bothered, rebuke them. Perhaps the disciples feel that an interruption by children is not appropriate for such an "adult" topic, but Jesus is indignant with the disciples for turning the children away.

The disciples had guessed Jesus' intent wrongly. In watching Jesus rebuke the disciples so often, you almost have to laugh. They kept having to swallow their pride and say, "Okay, we've learned our lesson—we won't do *that* again." This time they probably thought, "Jesus likes children, so we won't stop them from coming to Him, ever again!"

After Jesus says that the Kingdom of God belongs to such as these and declares that unless one receives the kingdom like a little child he won't enter it, Jesus blesses the children.

Next, Mark starts the story of the rich young ruler.

A little background helps understand this story. In that day people thought that wealth was a sign of God's favor upon an individual. By that standard, the young man in this story was highly successful and greatly blessed.

First, consider the connection between this story and the story Mark just told about Jesus and the children. Put yourself in the shoes of the disciples. They must have been thinking, "Jesus likes kids. We've got that figured out. Look, here's a young man who was a child only a few years ago and has turned out to be someone we'd like our own children to be like. He's polite, obviously religious, and interested in being saved! And he's rich, so he's blessed." I imagine they encouraged that young man to come to Jesus. They probably expected Jesus to say something nice to him and treat him favorably, just like the children. They never could predict what Jesus would do!

The young man begins, "Good teacher, what must I do to inherit eternal life?" (Wouldn't you want your kids to ask that?)

But Jesus replies, "Why do you call Me good? No one is good—except God alone."

Can you see the disciples muttering in dismay to each other? "Now why would He say that? Can't He see that this young man would be a good follower?" (It might also seem that Jesus was implying that He was not God. We will come back to this.)

Jesus continues by listing the commandments. The young man replies that he has kept them from his boyhood. Jesus looks at him and loves him. The young man was telling the truth. But then Jesus says a hard word. "One thing you lack. Go, sell everything you have and give to the poor, and you will have treasure in heaven. Then come, follow Me."

At this the young man's face fell. And he went away sad, because he had great wealth.

None of this made the slightest sense to the disciples. He turned away a good, religious, blessed young man with a staggeringly difficult demand. In our hoop terminology, He said, "You've jumped through a lot of hoops in your life. Here is a gigantic hoop: give away all you have to the poor!"

The disciples were amazed. If you look at the word *amazed,* it connotes not only amazement but also a gripping fear. Then Jesus made it worse. He said, "How hard it is to enter the kingdom of God. It is easier for a camel to go through the eye of a needle than for a rich man to enter the kingdom of God."

Even more amazed and fearful, the disciples looked at each other and asked (again in my hoop paraphrase) "Who then can be saved? If that polite, young man couldn't make it through that hoop—and I'm not as good as he is—then I certainly won't be able to make it through whatever hoop Jesus decides to put in front of me!"

Jesus answered, "With man this is impossible, but not with God; all things are possible with God."

Peter, looking for a ray of hope, said, "We've left everything to follow You." They had banked it all on Jesus. And Jesus responded that they had indeed made a wise investment.

Next Mark describes Jesus and the disciples on their way to Jerusalem. The disciples are still amazed and afraid about the issue of salvation. So He pulls them aside to talk to them privately. And what does the Master Comforter say to settle their fears and put their minds to rest? He tells them He is about to be betrayed, beaten, condemned and put to death. It goes from bad to worse!

Mark then finishes his Gospel with the story of Jesus' trial and crucifixion. Putting yourself in the disciples shoes, you can imagine that with Jesus' death, the disciples' hope— Jesus, the one person they clung to, was completely stripped away.

But then He rose from the dead! And, among other things, He foretold the coming of the Holy Spirit whom, He said, would bring all things He had told them to their remembrance. (John 14:26) And then Jesus ascended into Heaven and Pentecost came. Around this time, the disciples, as led by the Holy Spirit, must have started to comprehend all

those mysterious things that Jesus said in the previous
months, including the mystery of those three stories Mark told
in chapter ten.

Probably one of the first things they realized was why,
when they were so afraid and asked, "Who then can be
saved?" Jesus started telling them about His death. Hindsight
showed them that He really was answering their question. He
would save them through His death! When you think about
it, those three stories in Mark are all about how to be saved
and how not to be saved.

> **The story of the rich young ruler tells
> how not to be saved. His approach was
> by jumping through hoops.**

The first story, with the children, tells how to receive this
salvation: like a child, you just receive it trustingly. The story
of the rich young ruler tells how not to be saved. His
approach was by jumping through hoops. However, Jesus
showed him that he could never jump through enough hoops
to be saved. There is always another, higher hoop to jump
through. That's why Jesus asked why he called Him good
and said that no one was good except God. He wasn't trying
to tell him that He wasn't God or wasn't good. He was
saying, "You're looking for a good man to tell you that you
are good enough to be saved. And I'm telling you that there
is no one who is good, yourself included, except God. No
one is good except God. Don't look to yourself or your own
goodness for salvation. Look to God. That's who you need."
The third story, where Jesus predicted His death, tells what
accomplished our salvation. With man it was impossible. But
God made it possible. He jumped through the "ultimate"
hoop—and finished our hoop jumping forever!

Zacchaeus

The parallel account of the rich young ruler in Luke 18 is followed by the story of Zacchaeus. If anyone was a candidate to fail to get into Heaven, it was Zacchaeus! He was rich (remember what Jesus had just said about the rich) and, not only that, he was a tax collector. In those days, tax collectors were notoriously dishonest. They were Robin Hoods in reverse: robbing the poor to give to the rich— themselves. Most Jewish people considered them traitors because they worked for and supported the hated Roman occupation. He was rich, a sinner—and too short to jump through any hoops!

Zacchaeus was clearly one of the least likely men anyone would ever expect to receive the favor of God. So when he climbed up into a tree to get a better look at Jesus, the last thing he expected was that Jesus would have anything to do with him. He knew everything he had done—knowing there was not a single hoop he had ever jumped through, and that there was not much hope that he would ever jump through any hoops in the future. He would most likely have agreed how hard it was to enter into Heaven, but he was about to find out that with God anything is possible.

When Jesus looked up at him, He knew his name and called it out: "Zacchaeus." "Zacchaeus, come down immediately. I must stay at your house today."

In those days, saying that you were going to someone's home was tantamount to completely accepting him. That is why people would never enter the house of a sinner or tax collector. But grace had come, the amazing, saving, empowering grace of God, and Zacchaeus had received it, as evidenced by the fruit that followed and by the words of Jesus: "Today salvation has come to this house... For the Son of man came to seek and to save what was lost" (Luke 19:9-10). What the rich young ruler had sought but not received by jumping through hoops, Zacchaeus had now received by God's grace.

The people who saw this began to mutter, but Zacchaeus stood up and said, "Look, Lord! Here and now I give half of my possessions to the poor, and if I have cheated anybody out of anything, I will pay back four times the amount." Isn't it interesting that the very thing the rich young ruler was unable to do, Zacchaeus was doing freely, without ever being told to do so!

You see, the power to jump through hoops—and to gain God's salvation—comes from grace, not from the law. Comparing this story to the story of the rich young ruler, we see that they involve the very same hoop: the giving away of one's possessions. The law gave the rich young man no power to jump through the hoop Jesus put before him. He went away sad. But the grace offered to Zacchaeus gave him power, first to receive the acceptance of the Lord and then to jump through—without even thinking about it—this amazingly high hoop.

> **The law gave the rich young man no power to jump through the hoop . . . But the grace offered to Zacchaeus gave him power.**

All this is not to say that the law is useless. Far from it! The law has an essential use and power.

Defining Law and Grace

The law states what is right and wrong, what we should and should not do. It can carry a warning of the consequences of disobeying it, or news that we are in trouble—that we have sinned. Usually, the law starts with "You should" or "You should not." It can tell us to do good things (like pray) or to not do bad things (like not murder).

Grace is the amazing love and goodness that God gives us. The primary example of grace is God giving us His own Son that we might live. Grace and mercy are similar: grace is getting the good things we do not deserve; mercy is not getting the bad things we do deserve. Both are gifts at God's expense. Grace is about God—what He has done for us. The law is about us and what we have to do.

Although both law and grace are wonderfully deep topics to explore, these simple definitions give us a very practical way to distinguish which of the two (law or grace) we are using when we minister to people. When we are saying a "you should" sort of thing, it's the law. When it is "God is doing this for you," it is grace. It is important to know which we are using so we can understand the power involved and how to apply it to the ministry situation.

Both law and grace have a use and a misuse in ministry, and both need to be used correctly and at the right time. Scripture gives many examples of law being used when grace should have been offered. They are instances of legalism, condemnation and judgment (like the woman caught in adultery).

It is also possible to give grace inappropriately. Theologically it is called "unsanctified mercy." Telling people that a merciful God could not possibly punish sin or winks at moral failure are examples of this. Even giving mercy can be corrupted if we are giving it from our fallen nature. Misapplying grace may not be as common as misapplying the law, but it can happen.

The Purposes and Powers of Law and Grace

In describing the law's purpose, Martin Luther said that the law acts as a curb, a guide and a mirror. As a curb it restrains society. It informs the world that things like murder are wrong. As a guide, it shows us the best way to live our lives.

As a mirror, it shows us our true selves. It can show us that we are in sin, that we are in trouble, that we need God.

I think of the law's power as that of a knife. Hebrews 4:12 talks of the Word being "sharper than any double-edged sword; it penetrates even to dividing the soul and the spirit, joints and marrow. It judges the thoughts and attitudes of the heart." In Corinthians 3:1 it says that "The letter kills, but the Spirit gives life." That is the power of the law: it can cut, expose and kill. This can be very useful power in the right hands, but destructive in the wrong ones. Like a knife in the hands of a surgeon it can bring great good, cutting away things that can threaten our life; yet a criminal can wreak great harm with the very same knife.

In the wrong hands the law can condemn, not convict. I can use the power of the law inappropriately and see results by motivating people through guilt, but in the long run it will bear bad fruit. If I were to speak at a church about evangelizing, making everyone feel terribly guilty about not doing enough of it, I might pressure them into coming to a training course in evangelism, but they would not come with the right heart or the right motivation. Most likely that would filter through into the way they evangelized. When the results are accomplished through the power of grace and the Holy Spirit, however, people will also be motivated, but the fruit will be far better and more plentiful.

The purpose of grace is to save, heal, give life and draw us to God. It alone empowers us to do good.

Law and grace each have their own roles to play. The law then can pierce us, showing us our need for God.

Law and grace each have their own roles to play. The Father's heart is always to bestow grace and mercy, but until a person knows a need for God, coming to a point of brokenness in life, he or she cannot receive grace and mercy. "Why should I receive grace and mercy if everything's going fine in my life?" So the law then can pierce us, showing us our need for God.

Applications for Team Ministry

When to Use Law; When to Use Grace

• Remember that giving "you should" advice is in the realm of the law. It may be appropriate, but we must realize that the power to fulfill what we are suggesting is not in the suggestion itself. (This is one of the mistakes ministry teams can make—only giving "you should" advice instead of ministering the power found in what God is doing for us. We need to minister power.) That does not mean that we expect the person to be passive, doing nothing until God moves. The person may need to take a step, but make them aware that God's enabling grace will add power to any movement. For example, if a person is fighting temptation, I might quote James 4:7, "Resist the devil, and he will flee from you." With a little resisting, God will make the devil do a lot of fleeing. The resisting may be as simple as walking to a different location when temptation comes. Sometimes an action in the physical realm can affect where we are at in the mental realm. Then we can better receive God's power and revelation and arrive at a safe place.

• In seminary, we were told that our purpose was to "comfort the afflicted and afflict the comfortable!" That, simply put, is how to apply law and grace. If a person is in sin or trouble, they often already know it. The law has already done its work. There is no use in beating them over the head anymore. Jesus didn't preach repentance to Zacchaeus. He was obviously broken inside because salvation came to him. When Jesus encountered the woman at the well, He didn't berate her, though her sins were many. She was another who was ready for grace. However, the rich young ruler was comfortable, so Jesus ministered to him differently. When His disciples sometimes became a little arrogant, thinking they had vast amounts of faith, Jesus said, "O you of little faith; how much longer am I going to put up with you?" and challenged them to move on.

• It is generally safer to minister grace, especially when you are new in prayer ministry. In medical school, students are not allowed to do surgery without training and experience. They are not issued a scalpel and allowed to start cutting people their first year! Prayer ministers need training and experience, too. So while you are new at it, remain in the realm of grace. If you find it hard to remain in the realm of grace, perhaps because of the way you were taught or treated, get prayer and seek God that you might know first hand the power and depth of God's mercy and grace.

Administering the Law

• Know your leader's policies on ministering the law. Many teachers of the prophetic prohibit their trainees from giving directive words, corrective words or words that expose sins. Trainees are restricted to words of encouragement, exhortation and comfort. Some pastors and overseers of ministry teams always restrict their teams in this way. When a directive or corrective word is called for, their policy is to tell the leaders and leave appropriate actions to them. (At the very least, leaders need to establish some guidelines for their teams. For instance, giving words that publicly expose embarrassing sins or direct a person whom to marry should always be forbidden.) Respect your leaders' wisdom and guidelines. Otherwise you will not have the blessing of God.

• If you (or those in leadership) do need to minister the law, do it with a right heart—the heart of God. God loves people. Jesus loved us so much He was willing to die for us. Someone once said, "If you are not willing to die for a person, don't wound them." Also make sure you have the time, skill and commitment to see that any cut created with the law is healed.

• Be caring, sensitive and patient. Look at how patient God has been with you and me.

• Be accurate, like a surgeon. Don't exaggerate. Don't use words like "never" or "always" in describing what someone has done. Aim to win the person's restoration vs. winning a battle over convincing the person he or she is wrong.

• When you sense that sin is involved, it is often best to step out of a prayer or prophetic mode, if you are in one, and speak as one friend to another. God might prompt you to tell the person a story or share what He did with you. Stories (testimonies) are a non-threatening but powerful way to bring across a truth.

• If you need to minister the law, do it with a sense of desiring someone's freedom, not with a sense of condemnation. The person may experience conviction, but watch that they do not feel condemned. There is a real difference. The enemy uses condemnation, which always pushes the person away from God. God, on the other hand, uses conviction, which always draws us closer to Him. Isaiah 6 is a good example of conviction in action. In verse 1, Isaiah finds himself before God. Without the Lord saying a thing, Isaiah states, "I am an unclean man with unclean lips, coming from an unclean people." As is often the case, the presence of God alone was enough to convict. After Isaiah saw the Lord and his own uncleanness, God ministered grace—an angel took a coal off the altar and touched his lips, removing his sins. Then God said, "I need to send someone out. Whom will I send?" (my paraphrase) and Isaiah responded, "Here I am. Send me!" When God uses the law, He uses it with grace that empowers. We can do no less.

• When we need the law ministered to us—as a correction in our own lives—it will be easier to receive correction if we have friends with whom we are open. We need relationships with the freedom to share what is on our hearts and to speak into each others' lives. We must know we are completely for each other and want to do the best for one another, whether that means encouragement, apology or correction.

• While part of the law's purpose is to show us where we have fallen short, we must dissuade people from remaining so extremely inwardly focused and introspective that they miss out on the source of their help: God. Part of the key to sanctification is keeping our focus on what we want to become. We do not become holy by staring at ourselves. We look to Jesus and, through His grace, let Him empower us to change. We become like the One we dwell upon, and through following Him, He strips us of all that is not of Him and would hold us back. My friend George Koch once wrote, "Sanctification has more in common with holding on for dear life to the mane of a wild lion than it does with staring in the mirror and chanting, 'Every day, in every way, I am getting better and better.'"

• If you are being called into a position where you will occasionally minister the law, God will probably teach you how to combine law with grace by showing you how much you yourself need His grace. He will probably put you through all kinds of things to show you how desperately you need grace's refreshing, restoring power. He will also teach you that if you shoot the arrow of the law, you must shoot the arrow of grace right behind it to bring His healing. Then, your words will empower the person and give him power to change. Only after seeing how desperately we need grace are we ready to use the law's power.

Prophesying the Answer

John Paul Jackson, a man used effectively in the teaching and operation of the prophetic ministry, ministered to a friend of mine quite a few years ago. John Paul picked him out of a large crowd of people and spoke some remarkable things to him. During the prophecy, he referred to the struggles that constantly entrapped my friend, but did it in a way that encouraged and empowered him. "I see that you have these enemies . . ." and named them. "But the Lord is empowering you to come after these enemies so they won't distract you from your call any longer, and you will be able to overcome them and do the things that God has chosen you to do." When my friend got home, he was so excited and encouraged that he told everybody every detail! Furthermore, he had the power to overcome these things and change. It was wonderful to behold.

That's how to minister the law. The person doesn't feel "spanked," condemned and hopeless, just encouraged. He can respond, "God is for me. These things that have been holding me back can be conquered." Jesus said that He did not come to set aside the law (Matt. 5:17) and neither should we. In this verse He said He came to *fulfill* the law. He did so by bringing grace (John 1:14), grace to empower people to do the good things God wants done. So, too, when we minister, any words we give must also carry the power to fulfill them.

> **One of the most common mistakes ministry teams can make is to prophesy the problem but not the answer.**

In my opinion, one of the most common mistakes ministry teams can make is to prophesy the problem but not the answer (or to give too much attention to the problem and too little to the answer). They get the revelation but don't wait for the application—what God wants to do about the problem. Put yourself in the shoes of someone coming for ministry. If the minister gets a word of knowledge from the Lord about your problems or besetting sins and speaks it, you think, "I already knew that, and now I know God knows it and you know it, too. I'm worse off now than I was before!" There is no hope. If you get a revelation, don't share it right away. Take time to hear God's heart on it. Ask God, "Why are You telling me this? What are Your answers to the person's problems?" Sometimes it is not even necessary or wise to share the problem, only give the answer. They will know how to apply it without the shame of knowing you know all about it.

So don't just prophesy the problem; prophesy God's answers, which are always endued with His power-producing grace. When you prophesy the answer, those you are praying for not only know that God knows the problem, but also know that He cares and is on their side, offering to free them from whatever is holding them back. In ministering in this way, you are giving them an experience that is wonderfully encouraging and liberating, steeped with power to transform their lives. That is what our ministry should be about.

10
The Gifts of the Holy Spirit

When we think of a gift, we usually think of something we now possess, such as the watch someone gave us for our birthday. The watch can be used without the giver being present. That, however, is not so with the gifts of the Holy Spirit. The gifts do not operate without the presence of the Giver. Whenever a gift operates, the Holy Spirit is present, giving us the gift as we experience it. When Scripture speaks of the Spiritual gifts, the emphasis is on the here-and-now activity of the Holy Spirit as we are used by Him. Understanding this will help us experience and grow in the gifts and will keep our focus upon God.

This is illustrated in I Corinthians 12:1-7, preceding one of the major lists of various Spiritual gifts. In these verses, Paul describes what we refer to as gifts by using several different Greek words. In verse 1 the word is *pneumatikos,* literally translated "of the Spirit." In verse 4 it is *charismatos*, translated "gift freely and graciously given." In verse 6 it is a "working" which, Paul says, is *God* at work. In verse 7 it is a "manifestation of the Spirit." These descriptions point to a different concept than a gift which we possess independent of the giver. Rather, a Spiritual gift is about the *Spirit*—giving, working and manifesting Himself in us in a certain way for a certain purpose.

To generalize their purpose, the gifts of the Holy Spirit are tools for ministry given for the advancement of His Kingdom. For the most part, the gifts are given to us to benefit others (although they can also benefit us). Therefore, they are not only given *to* us, but are also gifts given *through* us to other people. Spiritual gifts are often experienced as God directing and enabling us to do something that is beyond our natural abilities. We may or may not be aware that it is God who is doing the directing and enabling, but a Spiritual gift is God supernaturally at work.

I use the word "supernaturally" to distinguish gifts from talents. Some activities, like creating music, may involve a gift or a talent (or both), while other activities, such as hearing God's voice, is a gift with no natural counterpart. Since both gifts and God-given talents have their source in God and both can be used for His service, there may be little practical need to draw a sharp line of distinction between the two. What we really need to know is how to recognize and use what God gives us so that we might fulfill what He is calling us to do for His kingdom.

Although I may describe some gifts more fully than others, I want to emphasize that all the gifts are important. Everyone in the Body of Christ is called to a specific part in the Lord's purposes. For every call, He supplies the gifts needed to carry it out. Just as everyone in the Body of Christ is important, so every gift is important.

Categorizing the Gifts

The following table of spiritual gifts is taken from the three primary references to gifts in Scripture: 1 Corinthians 12, Ephesians 4, and Romans 12, with the addition of a few other gifts mentioned elsewhere. Although the way I categorized some of the gifts may be debatable, for the most part they naturally fit under four headings: leadership (ministry) gifts, revelatory (prophetic) gifts, healing gifts, and service gifts.

Leadership Gifts

Apostle (Eph. 4:11, 1 Cor. 12:28)

Prophet (Eph. 4:11, 1 Cor. 12:28)

Evangelist (Eph. 4:11)

Pastor (Eph. 4:11)

Teacher (Eph. 4:11, 1 Cor. 12:28, Rom. 12:7)

Administration (1 Cor. 12:28)

General Leadership (Rom. 12:8)

Revelatory Gifts

Prophecy (1 Cor. 12:10, Rom. 12:6)

Wisdom (1 Cor. 12:8)

Knowledge (1 Cor. 12:8)

Discernment (1 Cor. 12:10)

Tongues/Interpretation (1 Cor. 12:10,28)

Encouragement (Rom. 12:8)

Creativity/Arts* (Ex. 35:30-36:1)

Music/Worship[†] (1 Chron. 15:16)

Healing Gifts

Healing (1 Cor. 12:9,28)

Miracles (1 Cor. 12:10,28)

Faith (1 Cor. 12:9)

Mercy (Rom. 12:8)

Freeing the Demonized[†] (Luke 9:1)

Counseling[†] (Prov. 15:22, 1 Chron. 27:32)

Peacemaker[†] (Matt. 5:9)

Service Gifts

Serving (Rom. 12:7)

Giving (Rom. 12:8)

Helping (1 Cor. 12:28)

Hospitality (Rom. 12:13)

Prayer/Intercession[†] (Col. 4:12, 1 Tim. 2:1)

Voluntary poverty* (1 Cor. 13:3)

Celibacy* (Matt. 19:11, 1 Cor. 7:7)

Enduring Persecution[†] (Luke 21:15)

Notes: * Said to be a gift, but not in one of the major lists of gifts

[†] Not mentioned as a gift per se, but a spiritual gift by virtue of the way it operates

Just as God speaks to us in many different ways, God employs an almost endless variety of spiritual gifts. I think the differences in the major lists in Paul's letters show that Paul was not trying to present an exhaustive list of gifts. He probably would have quickly acknowledged writing as a gift from God, but it is not included in any of his lists. As the conditions facing God's people change, God's creativity knows no bounds. He freely gives varieties of gifts to His people so that they may fulfill the call upon their lives. Just in looking at the production of a worship CD, it is clear that many different gifts are involved, some involving technologies (like sound mixing) which have been developed only recently. Granted, some of the excellence involved may be from natural talents, but the artists themselves often say that gifts supernaturally given by God were involved in the production of their works.

> ## I think the tendancy for the gifts to fall into these four categories conveys a message.

I think the tendancy for the gifts to fall into these four categories conveys a message. It shows that, while we may think that some of these categories are unimportant, God views each of them as very important.

Almost everyone recognizes the *leadership* gifts, which spearhead the ministries of the church, as important, especially when leadership is understood to include not only leading large numbers of people, but also small groups of people, families, and even single individuals.

Since one-fourth of the gifts are *revelatory*, it says something about their importance. The prominence of revelatory gifts may be surprising until we realize that no matter what we do for the Lord, it is critical to hear from Him. The revelatory gifts help us move in the other gifts—that is, the prophetic *empowers* the other gifts. In the 1980s when John Wimber brought a revelatory aspect to the ministry of healing, it resulted in a revival of the healing ministry. One of his central tenets (see Chapter Three) was based on John 5:19: "I only do what I see the Father doing." Figuring out what the Father is doing brings us back to the prophetic which, for John Wimber and the healing revival, empowered healing. When you can hear from the Lord, no matter what gift the Holy Spirit wants to use, you can do it more effectively.

Several years ago a friend of ours was baking bread and brewing coffee when she saw a street sweeper go past her house. She felt the Lord tell her to take some of the fresh bread and coffee to the driver. She dismissed it, thinking that she wasn't hearing right. When the sweeper went by her house again, once more she heard His familiar voice, but once again she dismissed it. About five minutes later, she heard Him again and finally began to think, "Maybe God is trying to tell me something!" So she cut a few pieces of bread, poured some coffee and went out to her car. By now the street sweeper was out of sight. She didn't know where it was, so she started crisscrossing the streets of her neighborhood in an attempt to find it. Finally she saw it, flagged the driver down and said, "You're going to think I'm crazy, but I was in my house baking bread and I felt the Lord tell me to go out and give this to you." The driver looked at her and asked, "Mrs. Lee, do you remember me? You used to be my Sunday School teacher."

She was astounded. She told him, "I didn't know the Lord back then the way I know Him now. I could tell you so much more about Him." They sat down and had a long talk. He told her how he hadn't been in church for a long time and felt he really needed God. By the end of the conversation, both were in tears. He was impacted that God cared enough about him to send his former Sunday school teacher out to search for him with fresh bread. It was a "divine appointment"— definitely a meeting brought about by the Lord. Hearing from God was an integral part of what happened. The gift of servanthood, coupled with the prophetic, produced empowered servanthood.

The attention given to gifts of *healing* may also be surprising to some, but God is a God who heals. And if healing includes emotional healing and spiritual healing (the healing of spiritual issues which separate people from God) as well as physical healing, then much of God's heart toward man is directed to healing. Having the heart of a healer, in everything we do, empowers us with the compassion that is central to the heart of God.

Considering the character of God, the prominence of *service* gifts is not at all surprising. He sent His Son in the form of a servant. In this century God has been sweeping His empowerment over every category of gifts: the leadership gifts, the healing gifts, and the prophetic gifts. It is my personal sense that this move of His power will not be over until He also empowers the servant gifts even beyond what we see now. Then we will see some of the most powerfully used gifts of all. Imagine empowered hospitality: the Lord will say whom to invite over, the guests will come and so will the Holy Spirit, and tremendous evangelism will take place in that home. The heart of a servant is essential for the proper employment of every gift and brings the true character of Jesus into any setting.

Steve Sjogren, in his book *Conspiracy of Kindness*, describes how he uses the gift of servanthood to effectively reach out to others. His teams often help the poor or go out on servant evangelism projects, such as raking people's leaves or shoveling their snow. When the home owners ask why they do this, they say it is just to show the love of God in a tangible way. They are not there to promote a church, only to promote a caring God. Such acts of kindness often naturally lead to sensitively asking if anyone needs prayer which often leads to the Holy Spirit coming in a powerful way.

No matter what call is upon our lives, leadership, revelation, healing and service are all important. In different ways, at one time or another, we are all called to lead. We all need to be prophetic—to communicate with the Lord. We all must have the heart of a compassionate healer. And we all must have the heart of a servant, no matter what our call is. Jesus is the ultimate example in each of these categories of gifts. He is the ultimate leader, the ultimate prophet, the ultimate healer and the ultimate servant. If we want to know how to operate in any gift, look to the way He did it. If our goal is to be like Jesus and do whatever He would do in the way He would do it, we will be using the gifts well.

The Levels of Use of the Gifts

Much of the confusion about the gifts of the Holy Spirit has arisen because we have not realized there are different levels in the ways the gifts are used. Rather than assigning names to these levels, I will just call them level one, two and three (and even talk about a level four).

At level one, anyone may experience any gift at any time. God may suddenly impart a gift to you that is just what is needed for the situation you are in. Maybe you have rarely, if ever, experienced that gift before and you may or may not regularly experience it in the future. It was there at a particular time for a particular purpose. Because this happens, everyone should be open to any of the gifts at any time, in whatever way God chooses. This makes ministering very interesting—you never know what God is going to do next!

At level two, you operate in a particular gift so often that it becomes your "specialty" or ministry. Usually you have a particular liking or affinity for being used in this way. Most people find it invigorating—not at all draining—to be used where they are called and gifted, an indication that this may be their specialty.

Level three is the office for the gift developed in level two. At level three, you are recognized and used by your church and others. In evangelism, for instance, we are all called to evangelize, and most of us can probably recall a time when the Holy Spirit imparted something to help us in this process (level one). For some, this happened so frequently that evangelism became their specialty or ministry (level two). We also know some who have operated in the third level—the office of evangelist—such as Billy Graham.

Where the lines are drawn between the different levels (especially between ministry and office) can be subject to debate. In reality there is a smooth transition between the levels (I may be at level 1.3 in one gift and 1.7 in another) and it really does not matter how they are delineated. This is certainly not about titles, rank or positions!!! Rather, the concept of levels helps us understand how the gifts operate and how we might grow in them—whether by being open to the gifts we have never before experienced or by seeking God for more depth in the ones we have experienced already.

Ephesians 4 talks about the offices of five of the gifts: apostle, prophet, evangelist, pastor and teacher. There is yet a fourth level for two of these which involves the authority to establish doctrine. The Old Testament prophets and the New Testament apostles were used at this fourth level to bring doctrinal truth into the church. Hebrews 1:1-2 says, "God, who at various times and in various ways spoke in time past to the fathers by the prophets, has in these last days spoken to us by His Son." In Old Testament times God used the prophets to bring the Word to the people and onto the written page. In the New Testament, now that the Son had come, we see God still using the prophets at the first three levels, but not at the fourth—they were not used to add to the body of doctrine. (See 1 Cor. 14:37.) Accordingly, the penalty for prophecies which missed the mark was very different between the Old and New Testaments (Compare the death penalty in Deut. 18:20 with 1 Cor. 14:29.) In the New Testament, the Holy Spirit used the Apostles to take the message and doctrine of Jesus and deliver it with purity to the church and to write it down to eventually be Scripture. Accordingly, we see somewhat of a spiritual "death penalty" for false apostles delivering wrong doctrine (Gal. 1:1-9). After the canonization of the New Testament, this fourth level was no longer needed—its task had been completed. However, the tasks associated with the first three levels have not—for apostles or prophets or any of the gifts. God gave us the gifts because He knew we needed them, and we need them now as much as ever.

It is important to recognize not only what the gifts look like at the higher levels, but also at the lower levels. At the first level, apostleship may look like a pioneering gift; perhaps a gift and desire to do things that have never been done before. It might involve going to places the Gospel has never been preached or planting churches. When this develops into the second level, it becomes a specialty, an overwhelming passion and desire. Growing toward the third level, there may be recognition by the church body for the fruit that has been poured out over the years, perhaps an appointment to oversee missions or to function in a fatherly role to the other pastors in a city or church affiliation.

Marriages of the Gifts

God is creative. He does not give His people just one type of gift, but a spectrum of them. His church is not a black and white snapshot; it is a living portrait filled with variety and color on every level. To add even more diversity to this picture, each specific gift operates in a variety of ways. In Scripture, some of the prophets were vision-oriented (Ezekiel), some were word-oriented (Jeremiah), some were given the task to anoint future leaders (Samuel), and some were called to a specific mission (Moses).

> **When the gifts are combined there are many fascinating marriages and blends.**

The same gift may operate quite differently in different people. Not only that, but when the gifts are combined—which God often does within individuals—there are many fascinating marriages and blends, adding even more diversity to the already colorful spectrum. For instance, the ministries of prophecy and intercession are by themselves interesting and powerful. But a whole new thing happens when they are merged and God gives you revelation of what to pray—things that could not be known through the natural realm. There are many powerful combinations of all of the gifts—evangelism and servanthood, prophecy and counseling, worship and evangelism. Combinations bring a new and powerful dynamic to both.

God may give combinations of gifts that we have not seen before. Sometimes it is best not to limit ourselves (or anyone) to the roles we see in today's church or world when trying to figure out where God is taking us. Our combination of gifts may make us feel like a square peg in a round hole until we figure out what He is calling us to do with them. It could be that we are gifted for a role that does not even exist yet— perhaps the world and the church have not yet arrived at the place where we can see what we were designed to do. Maybe we or someone else will create the role to which we were called. Then will our eyes be opened to see that we were born and gifted for a time such as this.

To illustrate how the gifts can work together and to highlight the importance of evangelism, here is a description of the reciprocal relationship between evangelism and the other gifts—first the effect of the gifts upon evangelism and then the effect of evangelism upon the other gifts. The gifts are given not only for edifying the church, but also to touch those who have not yet come to know Him. Used in this way, they carry a new aspect and power that is awesome to experience.

1. The Effect of the Gifts Upon Evangelism

When John Wimber introduced the topic of healing in his Fuller Seminary class (MC510: Signs and Wonders and Church Growth), much of it centered around a discussion of how evangelism and healing worked together. He had noticed in the mission field that whenever they were combined, the growth in the church was striking. When you think about it, evangelism and healing are a very natural combination. Conversations often begin with, "How are you?" (Step 1 in our prayer model) and often the people we're talking with tell us how they are doing. Then it is very easy to ask if we can pray for them. The results, even when you feel you have bungled it, are often that they know that you care for them, that God cares for them, and that God is real! When God does something during this kind of prayer, the people we are praying for often end up asking *us* questions about God. That makes evangelism a lot easier!

In Scripture it is amazing how often an evangelistic encounter is accompanied by a supernatural act of God, whether it is a prophetic word or a healing. (In fact, it is hard to find an evangelistic encounter in the Bible where a supernatural act was not present! I don't know of any!) This is not to say that other forms of evangelism are not useful and effective. All forms of evangelism (relational evangelism, apologetics, servant evangelism, etc.) are necessary and have their place. But healing and the prophetic are very powerful as evangelistic tools and should be given place as well.

> **Evangelism and healing are a very natural combination.**

A few summers ago my family and I were in northern Michigan visiting my mother. Her neighbor Dick, from two doors down, often came over to chat. He was a gruff sort of fellow, but very likable. He had fascinating stories about World War II. He was also an avid hunter—I think he had hunted every type of animal that ever walked the earth! He always had a pot of stew cooking on the stove, but most of us were afraid to ask what was in it!

That summer I noticed that Dick was very thin; not his usual robust self. We started talking and I asked how he was. He replied, "Oh, not so well." and told us he had a physical condition for which the doctor had given him a strong medication. That medication caused him to develop another condition, which I later found out was chronic diarrhea. It's bad when that lasts for a few days, but he'd had it over a year! He was losing weight at a rate of almost half a pound every day. There wasn't anything he could do about it; he could not go off the medication because of the severity of his primary illness.

We were interrupted at that point, but a few minutes later I told my mother that I felt that we should pray for Dick who, by this time, was wandering back to his house. She agreed, so we caught up with him and asked if we could pray for him. Thinking we just meant that we would keep him in our prayers, he said, "Sure" and headed into his house. But I told him that I meant we wanted to pray for him right then and there. So, slightly taken aback, he turned around and joined us.

One of the great things about having weekly ministry-training meetings in your church or home is that you get so used to praying for people that ministry seems to roll out of you in public. So, just as we had been doing in our meetings, we laid hands on Dick and asked the Holy Spirit to come, saying something like, "God, bring Your healing to Dick."

I didn't know what Dick was feeling, but I knew the Holy Spirit had come. As mentioned in Chapter Two, sometimes we can feel physical sensations of His presence. I didn't say anything about it, but as we prayed, it felt like wave after wave of gentle electricity. After praying just a minute or two, we finished, Dick thanked us, and we all went back to our houses.

A few days later we returned home. Curious about what had happened after praying with Dick, I went several weeks without hearing a thing. Then one day my mother said, "I talked to Dick today. It was amazing. He said that after we prayed with him, he started feeling much better. And instead of losing weight, he started regaining a pound every day or so. And he said that he knew it was the Lord who had done it."

I asked her, "How did he know that?"

She responded, "He said that when we were praying for him, he felt something like electricity all over his body, so he knew something had happened. And, from then on, he got better and kept gaining weight."

When Jesus ministered, He usually linked His works and His words: the proclamation of His kingdom went hand in hand with a demonstration of its effects upon this earth. Not being in the neighborhood, I pondered how I might have some sort of proclamation of who God was to go with this demonstration. So I wrote a letter to Dick. In thinking about it, I decided that I did not want to leave anything out, so it turned out to be a complete theological treatise on Christianity! This is not the recommended approach (like giving steak when a little bit of milk is called for—although, being a hunter, he did love meat!). But I sent it to my mother to give to Dick anyway. She, too, thought it was a bit much for him and confessed to me that she was relieved when he didn't open it in front of her.

We were curious how he would react but had to wait several more months before he finally mentioned the letter. Then one day, when my mother asked how he was doing, he said, "Much better! And if I do start feeling worse, I get out the letter about God and read it again, and then I feel better." Amazing!

The next summer, when our family went back to northern Michigan, I saw Dick again. Asking him how he was, he said, "Really well. I'm so much better now." Then he told me how severe his condition had become before we prayed and how he was now virtually free of both his primary condition and the resulting diarrhea. He went on, "It was interesting. Last fall I was out deer hunting with one of my buddies. He told me that he had just been diagnosed with cancer and I asked him if I could pray with him. You know, two days ago, the doctor gave him a clean bill of health!"

Sometimes I've tried so hard to teach people who have been long-time Christians how to pray for the sick and just cannot get through to them. But here is Dick out in the woods praying with his buddy, and doing it because he thinks it is normal—that it is what you are supposed to do! And you can be sure I'm not going to tell him any different! Praying for the sick and seeing them healed are *supposed* to be normative Christianity. It's the rest of us who have drifted away from the norm. As this experience showed me, when you bring people into the kingdom using the gifts of the Spirit, it becomes normative for them to also experience and use the gifts. They do it very naturally.

2. The Effect of Evangelism Upon the Gifts

Not only do the gifts of the Spirit enhance evangelism, but evangelism does something wonderful to the gifts. A few years ago I hosted a group in my home which focused on team ministry. After a year of training, we felt that we simply must take what we had learned "to the streets." We prayed for God to use us. Suddenly and amazingly, opportunities began to open up. We went to the homes of sick people, a shelter for homeless women, a place that fed Sunday dinner to the homeless. Our format in these places was usually the same as that of our home meetings: worship, a short teaching and ministry time. We found that the level of God's presence—to which we had become accustomed—overwhelmed the people in these places (and gave us a greater appreciation for it). I found that God's presence, the level of the gifts, and the level of anointings on our team members actually increased "out there." I call the phenomenon the "Great Commission Anointing" upon the gifts.

The people we reached out to were not the only ones touched. Some in our group who had been reserved suddenly found their niche and were being powerfully used by the Lord. And we were all making use of each other's gifts as a team.

On one occasion, for example, a team member felt that a young woman who was receiving prayer for healing was ready to receive the Lord. He quickly invited in another team member who was gifted in bringing Jesus to those who did not know Him and who happened to have a background similar to the woman receiving prayer. Afterwards, excited in realizing that this young woman had come to faith in the Lord, none of the team members would take any credit. They just honored one other and spoke of how each other's gifts had been used. A wonderful result of stepping out in ministry is that people can discover and begin to function in their callings and places in the Body of Christ. Whenever and whatever you give, the Lord gives back so much more.

Another consequence of being out there where "the rubber meets the road" is that team members began wanting answers to some tough ministry questions they encountered while ministering. We went on "outings" every other week but kept meeting in my home for worship and equipping on alternate weeks. The outings brought a new seriousness about being properly equipped as well as a wonderful sense of direction to the group. They also gave a new (and amazing) level of anointing to our meetings. The "Great Commission Anointing" is real and powerful!

Equipping the Saints

According to Ephesians 4:12, one function of the gifts of the Spirit is to equip other people to use them. If you are prophetic, one of your duties is to teach others to prophesy. In other words, one function of the prophetic is to make the church more prophetic. Even though many people might not consider the prophetic their ministry, your call is to teach and show them how to hear from God more effectively. That will help to empower whatever gift they are moving in. Similarly, one of the functions of the evangelist is to make the church more evangelistic, and so on. Whatever gift you move in, take someone by the hand, have them stand next to you while you're using it and show them how it goes. If they have questions, answer their questions. Then have them do it while you are there, and finally release them in it so they can do it alone and perhaps eventually teach others. That is the discipling process!

One of the best ways of imparting the gifts to others is through encouragement—acknowledging when someone has stepped out and attained a success. In my first semester of teaching at Valparaiso University, I was assigned to teach a calculus (advanced mathematics) class for non-mathematics majors. Calculus is a subject that can strike fear into any student's heart! Knowing the power of encouragement, I decided to try an experiment: I would make my first quiz extremely easy to bolster the students' confidence and then see what happened. As the sweaty-palmed students sat down at their quizzes, you could see amazement in their faces when they realized they could do it! Handing back their papers marked mostly with A's and B's, some commented, "Wow, I didn't know I could learn calculus!" I made the second quiz a little more challenging, but to my surprise, their confidence was so high that they continued to get excellent grades. Each quiz I made harder until the class was at the normal level of difficulty, but the students continued to get A's and B's—and liked math! Now I had a problem—the university expected professors to give an average grade of perhaps a little over a C. That was *much* lower than the average of my class. So I made the quizzes and tests even harder, but they continued to do well! (That was a problem every teacher wishes for!) This demonstrates the power of encouragement. I don't feel I am exaggerating when I say that it changed the outlook of some of those students for life. One even became a math major. And if encouragement could do that for a math class, imagine what it can do for our God-given mandate to impart the gifts to our fellow believers. Even if you feel that you don't yet know enough to teach (which is probably not true— everyone can teach *something* they have discovered), there is much you can impart through sincere encouragement.

Love and Unity

It is interesting that each section of Scripture which lists Spiritual gifts is either immediately preceded or followed by a section about love. The list of gifts in Romans 12:6-8, for example, is followed by the discussion about love in Romans 12:9-21.

Two of the greatest chapters on gifts are 1 Corinthians 12 and 14. In between them is 1 Corinthians 13—perhaps the most well known chapter on love. Paul put chapter 13 there for a reason. As I've emphasized throughout this book, if you do not have the heart of God and cannot be used in the gifts of the Spirit with love, it is best not to do them at all.

Someone once pointed out that 1 Corinthians 13:4-7 can be a profound instruction on the use of the gifts. Try substituting a spiritual gift for the word love. "The prophetic is patient, the prophetic is kind; it is not jealous." The key is that prophesying, healing, helping or leading is never about you; it's always about wanting the best for the other person. Every single one of the qualities and instructions Paul gives about love applies to the use of the gifts. In 1 Corinthians 12-14 Paul is painting a picture of the entire church flowing in their different gifts, with love as the glue that holds them together. It all hinges on love; it all hinges on unity.

Paul underscores love and unity once again in the verses both before and after his discussion of the five leadership gifts (apostle, prophet, evangelist, pastor and teacher) in Ephesians 4:11-12. Ephesians 4 is an interesting portion of Scripture, highlighting both the unity of the church and the diversity of the gifts. It is saying that unity and love are needed to move in the diversity of the gifts. And it also is saying that the diversity of the gifts actually produces unity in the church.

So how does diversity produce unity? Diversity makes us need each other. I might be praying for a person who has yet to know the Lord and I don't know how to effectively proceed. I might wish I had a person who specialized in evangelism to help and suddenly another team member with the gift of evangelism arrives to share in the ministry. Our need and appreciation for one another joins us together in ministry to function as one. That is diversity producing unity. The love and respect for other team members and their various gifts is what makes this type of diversity possible in the first place. That is unity enabling diversity.

Ministering With the Gifts of the Spirit

As I said in Chapter Eight, the tips for ministering prophetically apply to all the gifts of the Spirit. In this chapter I will add to that list some tips that apply to ministering with the variety of Spiritual gifts.

• As you are engaged in team ministry, be open to the variety of gifts that God may use in you. Remember that He can use any gift at any time. Also be open to how He may use the gifts that are in other people. It is a delightful experience to see how the different gifts God has given each of us can fit together in a ministry situation. Like a team sport, it is very satisfying when everyone has a part to play in a victory.

• Don't base your self worth on your gifts or on what you do, but on who you are in God. Be a worshipper of Him. Don't seek gifts in order to be more accepted by man or to be more loved by God; thrive on the love God has already established for you. God declared, "This is my Son, whom I love; with Him I am well pleased." (Matt. 3:17) He said that before Jesus even began His ministry, before Scripture records that He did one miracle or used one gift. That is how God loves and values us, as well.

• Be open to the supernatural, but don't think of yourself as second class when supernatural things do not seem to be happening. They often come in waves and seasons. Besides, it is not always the overtly supernatural things that happen that touch God's heart. His heart is touched when we express His love. The supernatural element of what we do is up to God, who is full of surprises, no matter what our gift.

• Don't take yourself too seriously, thinking of yourself as being in an exclusive club. Be open and accessible, inviting others in the joy of being used.

• Perhaps the most useful tip is that, as we minister, it is best not to keep our eyes on the gifts, but on God the giver. When I was on a ministry trip at a wonderful church in the Dominican Republic, the pace they set for us was grueling. For about 14 hours a day we were engaged in team ministry, with the exception of a few breaks and being refreshed by some of the most awesome worship I have ever experienced. This pace went on day after day for about 8 days. After a day or two, being dead-tired, I wondered if my weariness would affect the flow of the gifts. It did not. (After all, they are *gifts*.) But the biggest lesson I learned was that if I even started down the road of thinking, "How are my gifts doing today?" the gifts diminished. However, if my focus was entirely on love for the people to whom we were ministering, on God and on the enjoyment of His presence, then the gifts always flowed in great abundance. Therefore, as you set out in ministry, don't focus on how well your particular gifts are doing at the moment. Focus on the people and on God. The Holy Spirit may not even give us the gift we need until we need it. The ministry we are talking about has been likened to a carpenter walking into a workplace with an empty toolbox—it doesn't contain a single tool! But as the need comes, you reach in, and sure enough, the exact tool you need is right there. Admittedly, this can make you a little panicky when you first start, but it is also exhilarating as you reach in and there it is, time after time. This process develops a dependency on and a relationship with God. The gifts are God at work. It is His ministry, and He is giving us the privilege of partnering with Him in it. Though each gift is very valuable and fascinating, our focus must be on Him, whose heart is rich in love and compassion for whom we pray and endued with power that the will of His heart may be done.

> **If my focus was entirely on love for the people to whom we were ministering, on God and on the enjoyment of His presence, then the gifts always flowed in great abundance.**

• Although I have mentioned this before, it bears repeating that we must not pursue gifts or power and exclude pursuing God Himself and holiness. Do not go down this road, even a little. Without holiness, the ministry which we so eagerly seek will eventually blow up in our face. In *God's Generals—Why They Succeeded and Why Some Failed*, Roberts Liardon wrote about men and women of the past century who were powerfully used by God. Roberts wanted to be very open about their successes and failures. It highlighted the importance of holiness and character issues which we may be tempted to put on the back burners, but that can make the difference in the long-time effectiveness of ministries. Another work which drives this point home is Rick Joyner's *The Final Quest*. There is something about this book that can crucify the wrong motivations we have for ministry and purify the correct ones, vital for anyone becoming involved in ministering to others.

If our heart is on God and on His heart for people, He will give us what we need when we need it. If I did not say ministering in the gifts was fun, I would not be honest. The gifts are really putting us in the role of postmen: bringing packages from God to those to whom we minister, and it is a thrill to watch people receive them.

Even though we may picture the gifts of the Holy Spirit as tools for ministering, the truer picture is that we, in our diversity, are tools in the hands of the Lord which He may use at will. Be ready to be used by the Lord and picked up out of His toolbox as He has need of you. And, in whatever way He chooses to use you, let Him equip you with the appropriate gifts so that His glorious will may effectively be done.

11

The Second Reformation

I am convinced that there is a God-given journey for each of us, a vision to fulfill, a part to play in the cause of Christ and the perfect giftings to use along the way. In other words, upon each of our lives is a *call*.

Discovering our call can come in an instant (like Paul on the way to Damascus), but often it comes in stages as we amass more and more clues and confirmations. Sometimes looking at the gifts we often employ, as well as our talents, personalities and heart-felt desires, gives us a clue about our call. Often we have only a general sense of what our call is, just enough to act on, and the details are filled in later. While it is important to discover our call, we must not become so future-oriented (or self-oriented) that we ignore what God is doing every day. We must not ignore the fact that the journey is sometimes as important as the destination. It is often the things we do and the people we touch along the way, sometimes through unforeseen circumstances, that make the most powerful impacts for God's kingdom. It may be that these things we are doing are, or will lead us to, our call. Therefore we must not overlook the journey in lieu of looking for our destination. Yet it is also true that having a sense of our destination can help us prepare and plan ahead. Also, looking farther down the road can help us keep going straight in God's path and not get bogged down in bumps or distractions. So pray God would show you *both* today's journey and tomorrow's destiny.

When I talk to Christians, I am astounded by how many of them have an incredible sense of the journey that He is sending them on. Some may have the excitement of discovering this still ahead of them, but I am convinced that God has a journey in mind for every one of us. Looking at what God is speaking to one individual is amazing in itself, but thinking about how the journeys of all God's people are going to fit together is even more astounding—God seems to be up to something big! For Him to accomplish this, the church will have to be a place which not only encourages and equips all believers in their calls, but utilizes them and installs them into a vast army with Christ as the head. What we are talking about—the journey ahead for the Church itself—is tantamount to nothing less than a Second Reformation.

Ephesians 4

The first reformation, in Martin Luther's day, brought grace and Scripture into the hands of the people. The second reformation, which is yet to come, will bring *ministry* into the people's hands. The truths underlying both the first and second reformations are clearly drawn out in Scripture. The first reformation was built on Ephesians 2:8 "For it is by grace you have been saved through faith—and this not from yourselves, it is the gift of God." The idea of the second reformation is drawn from Ephesians 4 which begins, "I [Paul], therefore, the prisoner of the Lord, beseech you to walk worthy of the calling with which you were called, with all lowliness and gentleness, with longsuffering, bearing with one another in love, endeavoring to keep the unity of the Spirit in the bond of peace." (Eph. 4:1-3, NKJV) Its starting point, therefore, is combining our call with a servant's heart: a heart for love and unity.

Ephesians 4:11 continues by describing the gifts Jesus gives the church, "And He Himself gave some to be apostles, some prophets, some evangelists, and some pastors and teachers..." (NKJV) The five gifts mentioned here are often called the "five-fold" ministry gifts, although some say it is only four-fold because pastor and teacher are combined. Whether it is four or five, the important thing is that it speaks of a diversity—a spectrum—of calls and gifts.

Then, in verse 12, Paul tells the reason for the gifts, "for the equipping of the saints for the work of ministry, for the edifying of the body of Christ..." (NKJV) This is the Second Reformation: that the saints—every believer—may take part in the work of the ministry.

He concludes in verse 13 with the final goal, "till we all come to the unity of the faith and of the knowledge of the Son of God, to a perfect man, to the measure of the stature of the fullness of Christ." (NKJV) The product of the diversity of gifts and calls is unity. It takes unity to produce them, but having them produces even more unity.

The term *five-fold ministry*, may either set off alarms or enthusiastic responses in people's minds depending upon their past experience with the terminology. Just to be clear, I am *not* talking about who controls the church! Church government is an interesting subject, but I am talking about something else. Please don't let externals, like the language people use to describe themselves or the structure of their church, be the measure of how closely they have come to the Second Reformation. I have heard church leaders use Ephesians 4:11 terminology to describe their ministry, when in reality they are closer to "one-man shows" than they are to bringing ministry into the hands of the people. On the other hand, I know of liturgical churches with traditional forms of government that come as close to the ideals set forth in this chapter as any churches I have seen. The difference is in the hearts of the leaders and the people.

> **I am not talking about
> who controls the church.**

To me what is profound in these verses is the simple fact that there is a diversity of gifts and a call on every person in order to be part of Jesus' ministry here on the earth. It is making us need one another; it is making the Body of Christ fit together.

It is sad, however, that the church so often takes their people and their gifts and simply sets them on a shelf. In contrast to the picture of diversity and vitality described in Ephesians 4, we have too often settled for a picture of dusty jars upon shelves. If we were able to take these people and their gifts off their shelves and start using them, we would be astounded at what would happen. That is what Ephesians 4 is all about: bringing the members of the body of Christ off the shelves and starting to use them. That is God's heart. That is the coming reformation.

The Second Reformation

John Stott spoke of such a reformation in *The Message of Ephesians*. He said, "If the sixteenth century recovered the 'priesthood of all believers' (every Christian enjoying through Christ a direct access to God), perhaps the twentieth century will recover the 'ministry of all believers' (every Christian receiving from Christ a privileged ministry to men)." He also said, "For clearly the way the whole body grows is for all its members to use their God-given gifts. These gifts are so beneficial both to those who exercise their ministry faithfully and to those who receive it that the church becomes steadily more healthy and mature" (p.168).

In Chapter One I mentioned how I would stand and look at the statue of Martin Luther, thinking how badly a second reformation was needed. Years later, when I saw the Holy Spirit empowering people to effectively minister to others, it suddenly hit me that, as awesome as that was in itself, God was up to something bigger than we even realized. Part of a new, a second, reformation had snuck upon us unaware. Yet I knew that this was only the beginning—it would take perseverance to hold onto what we had and to cling to the hope that it would come to its fullness. I didn't (and still don't) know what the Second Reformation will look like in its fullness—all I can sense is that there is more, and that God yearns for it.

Several years ago, I happened to be teaching on Ephesians 4. Just before the meeting began, someone looked out the window and saw a patch of color in the sky. All of us ran outside for a closer look and realized that we were actually seeing five rainbows (or segments of rainbows), side by side, each with a full spectrum of colors. I have never seen anything like it before or since; I have seen double rainbows, but nothing like this. After they had faded away, we went back inside for our meeting. After worship and our discussion of Ephesians 4, someone commented, "It's interesting Paul mentions five gifts and we saw five rainbows." Then it hit me. That was exactly what we had been talking about! There is a broad spectrum of gifts, each gift itself with a spectrum of uses and combinations. To me the rainbows were a demonstration of God's heart, saying, "This is My heart for the church. I want my church to be seen in her beauty and glory—that everyone who is a part of her, who has their own part to fill in this beautiful spectrum, would come together and that she would become everything that I've called her to be." I thought then that I had no idea how God would do it, but I sure would love to see it done. If the rainbows we saw were beautiful, how much more so would be the Church.

The Moving "V"

Several years before seeing the rainbows, I was at a pastor's conference and, during one of the sessions, I saw a picture in my mind superimposed over the physical scene. It looked like a sideways 'V' moving from left to right. It reminded me of a flock of geese flying in "V" formation or the wake of a moving boat. This "V" was moving across the world, across the lost. The "V" was the front line of the church. Superimposed on the "V" were all the various gifts.

At the point of the "V" were apostles; they were directing where the "V" should go—uncharted territory where it was called to go next. On one leg of the "V" were evangelists; they were right on the line because they were reaching the lost as this moving "V" encountered new people. The prophetic were on the other leg, because one of the main functions of the prophetic is evangelism (1 Cor. 14:24-25).

Just behind the "V" were the teachers. As the lost came in, the teachers would instruct them in the different elements of the faith. It was an intensive time of discipling, showing new believers what Christianity is all about. (It is interesting to note that the "Alpha Course" developed in England a few years ago, has just this vision.)

Behind the teachers were several waves of pastors. The first were taking the newly saved and gathering them in small groups where they would be taught and cared for. Other waves of pastors were overseeing their pastoral care; they were bringing people into fellowship with Christians in larger settings and networking them with Christians in the greater Body of Christ.

Throughout the "V" were intercessors. They were lobbing "bombs" up ahead of the front lines to soften the ground as the "V" moved forward.

And there were healers. As the lost would come in, it was critical that there be healing offered to them. The need for healing was, and is, at epidemic proportions—one out of four girls and one out of eight boys, for example, will have been physically abused by the time they reach age 18. And these numbers only reflect physical abuse—how many more must be affected by verbal abuse? Or how many are living with drug or alcohol abuse within their immediate family? (The statistics say one out of every four.) Everything is at epidemic proportions. As the lost come in, those God will use in the ministry of healing are vital, both on and behind the front lines.

Each of the gifts on the "V" had an equipping function, too. As people were incorporated into the Body of Christ, they would be trained by equippers so that they would come into their own gifts and callings and take their own place on the moving "V."

All the gifts fit amazingly well into this picture. Servanthood, hospitality, worship, and the like interweaved beautifully into the overall design as the "V" encountered the lost. As I was seeing this picture, the Lord was showing me how vital each gift is. It is important to realize this when you think that some gifts are emphasized more than others—you might be tempted to feel that your particular gift is "lower class" compared to another, or you might not know where yours fits in. But when you finally see the bigger picture and how everything fits, you will come to realize that you, too, have a place in the work of God's kingdom. When this "V" moved across the world, it struck me how every gift had a place.

The odd thing about watching this was that as soon as the "V" stopped moving, it disappeared. When a boat stops moving, the wake disappears, or when geese stop flying, their formation disperses. When this "V" stopped moving, no one knew what to do with many of the people or their gifts. But once the church started moving again, the "V" formed and everyone had a place. The "five-fold" ministry (that is the variety of gifts and calls) is designed to work in something *moving*—if it is not moving it is an exercise in frustration to try to make everything fit in.

> **The "five-fold" ministry (that is the variety of gifts and calls) is designed to work in something moving.**

The "Second Reformation" is not just a catchy phrase or something that might be nice to watch take place. We absolutely need it. Those who study church growth have said that if the professional church leaders alone did the work of the church, the church could do little more than maintain the status quo. For the church to grow, it is necessary for everyone to take part. I think there is such a harvest coming that this is becoming more and more urgent. I think this is why churches of every stripe are being awakened by the Spirit of God who is saying, "The people need to be equipped. Something is coming. Get ready. Be prepared. It is imperative." It is significant how many people are hearing that these days. Ephesians gives us a blueprint for how it can happen.

Our Attitude Must Change

When the diversity of gifts and the ministry of all believers described in Ephesians 4 does not happen, some people blame church leadership—and sometimes they are right, the leaders are at fault. Sometimes leaders feel that it takes less time and energy to do everything themselves rather than go through the bother of training others. Some feel they simply do not have the time or talent to train others. Some feel insecure, that they will not be needed if other people are doing the ministry. However, much of the blame lies in the attitude of the people themselves. So often our expectation is that, "Someone else will do it. It's their job. They are trained for it. It's their thing." We have willfully taken the role of spectators. But Christianity was never designed to be a spectator sport. Never!

An attitude that may inhibit the Second Reformation even more than these, however, is the thirst in the Church to watch a John Wayne type (or more specifically, the characters he played), a self-sufficient do-it-all super-hero, do everything himself. I remember seeing an advertisement which went something like, "Come see Brother So-and-so move in all nine gifts of the Spirit." When I saw that I thought, "I would much rather see nine different people, each with their own gifts, moving together in the Spirit! That would be the real miracle!" Better yet, I'd like to see an entire army of believers moving in the gifts of the Spirit all together, all in harmony. Not until we, as the people of the church, truly hunger for everyone to be used and are satisfied with nothing less, can we blame others for the lack of a second reformation?

The attitude of the church has got to change. There must be leaders. God anoints people for leadership and strong, persistent leaders are necessary for the Second Reformation. But we must have the heart to see that everybody does the work of Jesus. Part of our dream must be to see other people's dreams come true. My heart is to see everyone moving like Jesus did. I want to see millions and millions of Jesuses out there doing the things He did and saying the things He said. Be aware that the enemy takes special aim at this vision and the people who hold it. It is extremely threatening to him. So when you see a church or people with this vision in their hearts, please pray for them. Ask God to protect what He has begun.

> **Part of our dream must be to see other people's dreams come true.**

I am under no illusion that all this will be easy. I have encountered problems, first hand, to which there are no easy answers. There will be imperfections and abuses—leaders who will use the language of Ephesians 4:11 to demand submission instead of earning respect. There will be people who will use these concepts as an excuse to overthrow their pastors (which is clearly opposite the spirit of Ephesians 4!). There will be leaders—as well as the people they are trying to lead—who are threatened by new ideas. There will be people who demand to be promoted before they are ready to handle the responsibility. It takes people who are willing to serve, to try out their dreams on a smaller scale, and to go through whatever pruning, trials, perseverance, training and character-building the Lord puts them through first. Sometimes this takes time (I know it did with me). There will be those who try to accomplish this reformation with human strength rather than by the Spirit. There will also be people who do not want to serve anymore because they were burnt out in the past through overuse, often in jobs that came with too little support or that were designed by visions which they did not really own. (See *The Other Side of Pastoral Ministry* by Daniel Brown for valuable advice on utilizing people and their gifts. This book may give more practical steps for moving towards a second reformation than any I've seen.) In general, as we start down the road of launching people into ministry, there will be messes to clean up. But as it says in Proverbs 14:4, "Where there are no oxen, the manger is empty [KJV: clean], but from the strength of the ox comes an abundant harvest." So which do we want? A clean stall or an abundant harvest? We must remember that the goal is *God's* idea and desire not ours, and that He has a plan for making the seemingly impossible become a reality, if only we would try.

Promising Signs

Recently there have been many promising signs and movements towards incorporating people and their gifts into the ministry of the church. In the Lutheran church and others, there are very popular programs to equip lay ministers. In many denominations, the small group movement is multiplying the pastoral and teaching gifts among the people. As mentioned before, the Alpha Course is multiplying the teaching and evangelistic gifts. Billy Graham and other well known evangelists are combining the evangelistic and pastoral gifts by coupling their evangelistic crusades with the pastors and people of local churches. John Paul Jackson is combining the prophetic gifts and evangelism with extraordinary results, sending out teams to minister to people outside the church. The Vineyard and other movements have done much to equip the saints, incorporating them into a variety of ministries like praying for the sick and helping the poor. But even John Wimber, who led many churches in this direction, saw some of them drifting away from this vision. In speaking to a gathering of pastors he said: "I thought, 'My God! We've made an audience out of them. And they were an army!' We in effect told them, 'You can't do anything. You aren't talented enough. You're not gifted enough. You're not holy enough. You're not prepared enough. Stand back and let somebody who is do it!' We did it, not so much by precept, but by example." (*John Wimber, The Way It Was*, pp. 180-181). (Now, more than ever, I appreciate how much John Wimber's heart beat to see everyone ministering.) No matter what our denomination and no matter how far we have progressed in the vision of equipping the saints for the work of the ministry, it takes determination and perseverance by everyone to keep on that track.

I long for the fullness of the Second Reformation. Yes, there are many promising signs, but we have not yet arrived. I want to see the moving "V"! I want to see each person fulfilling his or her dream and the Church colored by a spectrum of gifts. There must be more! There has *got* to be more if we are to meet the challenge God has set before us.

When I began to write this book, I felt I was to write about Spirit-empowered ministry taking place in teams and the Second Reformation, but the combination seemed odd. The concept of a reformation seemed so grandiose that talking about ministry teams became small-scale by comparison. Yet, it is at the level of two or three coming together—agreeing to believe God and moving out in His presence—where much of the Second Reformation will take place. And the teams' ministry will not always be within the four walls of the church. It was not there in the Book of Acts, and the Second

Reformation will once again push the ministry into the everyday world. Much of the supernatural activity of God will be in homes, businesses, retirement centers and the marketplace. The concept of where the work of the church takes place will be broadened beyond the walls of church buildings to wherever God's people go. We will still enjoy the celebration and nurturing that takes place in large church meetings, but the work of the royal priesthood will be everywhere.

> **The teams' ministry will not always be within the four walls of the church.**

The Magnificent Journey

If what countless people are sensing about their future journeys is true, to fulfill them all, the Second Reformation will have to take place. And we will see the Church become transformed beyond our imaginations. As God causes the Church to recognize that no person's journey can be ignored, it will become a place that will inspire us in our quest to know God, empower us to fulfill our callings, and join us together to build the Kingdom like never before. And we will see how our journeys really fit together into the one magnificent journey of the Church herself.

In Ephesians 4, after talking about the gifts, Paul says, "Speaking the truth in love, we will in all things grow up into Him, who is the head, that is, Christ. From Him the whole body, joined and held together by every supporting ligament, grows and builds itself up in love, as each part does its work." (Eph. 4:15-16). This is the true vision of the Church. Like a living body, it is growing and connecting together as we, the necessary ligaments, are coming into place, each doing the work we were meant and privileged to do. In a human body it is the head that both gives us our identity and decides what we do and say. So it is with the Body of Christ—Jesus is our Head. We will look like Him, think like Him, work like Him and talk like Him. As we become more like this picture of the church described in Ephesians, the world will recognize *Him* as they see the Church. That's what He has always wanted—Him in us and us in Him and all of us in such unity that the world may know God has sent the Son (John 17:23). Not only will we look like Him, but we will have Him with us—where even two or three are gathered together in His name, Jesus is among us (Matt 18:20). And where Jesus is, anything can happen.

Moving Towards a Second Reformation

Because I have not experienced the Second Reformation in anywhere near its fullness, it is with some reticence that I offer tips about how to move towards it. Nevertheless, I do know some heart attitudes are essential.

• Seek God. Seek God. Keep seeking God.

• Have a heart for unity in the church, yet a delight in the diversity of people and their spiritual gifts. Pray and earnestly desire that all the people and all their gifts be used.

• Seek to be filled with His Spirit and used by Him. Become equipped. Equip others.

• Be open to being used outside the four walls of the church. Wherever you go, ask the Father to show you what He is doing.

• Have a servant's heart.

• Have a heart that is full of faith, ready for adventure, willing to do even what looks impossible.

• Make part of your dream be for the dreams of others to come true.

Arrows in His Hands

My purpose in this book has been to equip you, to give you arrows, if you will, so that when you go out to minister, your quivers may be full. You may pull out the arrow of faith, the arrow of grace, or any one of the arrows of the gifts of the Holy Spirit. My purpose has also been to let you know that, if your quiver seems empty, the Holy Spirit is with you—we partner with Him in *His* ministry—and He will put arrows in your quiver as you have need.

In 2 Kings 13, Elisha placed some arrows in the king's hand and told him to strike the ground. The king struck the ground three times. Elisha said, "You should have struck the ground five or six times; then you would have defeated Aram [your enemy] and completely destroyed it. But now you will defeat it only three times." He was pointing out that we must *persist*. Our persistence will produce fruit.

Yes, God gives us arrows, but we are also arrows in His hands. And those arrows were made to be used. Pastors, we must realize that we are not the only ones who should experience the thrill of being used. We must fulfill the dreams of others. Every believer has a destiny to be "built into a spiritual house to be a royal priesthood, . . . a holy nation, a people belonging to God, that [they] may declare the praises of Him who called [them] out of darkness into His wonderful light" (1 Peter 2:5,9). The privilege of partnering with God, feeling His heart beat within ours and taking His words and His works to a world which desperately needs them, is a privilege God has purposed to share with *everyone* in His Church. It is for this purpose that we are like arrows in His hands. As we are shot from His bow, sailing through the air to our target, we have to admit that there's no adventure quite like the one we are on.

That's why we cry out to God, "We will follow You wherever You go! Do with us, Lord, what You will, as long as Your presence goes with us." Let it so be with us, the Church, as we continue on our magnificent journey, following the Lamb wherever He goes.

APPENDICES

A. Ministry Times: What We Value

During our ministry times we desire our ministry to be:

1) **FATHER-CENTERED.** Like God the Father, we want to care for each person with His love and compassion—that of a father towards his child. We want them to know that God is here and that He cares.

2) **JESUS-CENTERED.** We want to focus on Jesus—His presence, person, character and acts on our behalf. We know that if our focus is elsewhere, like Peter, we will sink into the sea.

3) **SPIRIT-CENTERED.** We desire to be led by the Spirit as completely as possible. We are often quiet to hear His voice, sensitive to His promptings, prophetic words and giftings, and desirous to move in His presence, power and anointing.

4) **WORD-CENTERED.** Everything we do must be Scriptural. The counsel and power of the Word we hold in high esteem.

5) **PERSON-CENTERED.** We must always listen carefully to the person to whom we are ministering. We must respect his or her dignity. We want to be confidential about what they share, respectful and sensitive.

6) **LEARNING-CENTERED.** We want to be teachable. We don't want to "take over" ministry times, but want the Holy Spirit to use everyone on the team and let everyone grow in ministry. Although the Spirit may heavily anoint one person in a given situation, we believe He wants to raise us all up in the ministry and, at different times, will anoint each one of us to take part. For one person to take over a ministry session (especially a newcomer who does not know what we are doing and wants to "show everyone how to do it") without the express permission of the group leader is out of godly order.

7) **INTEGRITY-CENTERED.** Integrity, openness and honesty are very highly valued. In giving prophetic words, we need to be honest in what we say God is speaking to us and how certain we are He is saying it. In reporting healings, we must always be honest and not exaggerate. There will be times the healings we pray for do not take place—we must be open about it and offer to pray at another time, being careful not to place a burden of failure on the person for whom we pray.

B. Sample Guidelines for Ministry Teams

1. It is often a good idea to have at least one person on the prayer team with the same gender as the person you are praying for. If the topic of prayer is personal or if you are meeting in a private setting, this is very important. Find someone of the appropriate sex to join your team. In some sensitive situations, it may be better that no one of the opposite sex minister.

2. Avoid inappropriate touch or getting too close when ministering to someone of the opposite sex. Be sensitive to women who have been sexually abused—any touch whatsoever by a man may make them so uncomfortable that it shuts down their receptivity to what God is doing in prayer. Generally touch is very comforting and healing to a person, but sometimes it may be intrusive. Therefore, it is often best to simply pray with your hand a few inches above the person's head until you find out which is the case.

3. The things people share with you during ministry time should be kept confidential. The only exception is when there is danger to someone's life (the person is suicidal, is a victim or perpetrator of physical abuse, etc.). Then let one of the leaders know immediately.

4. Don't give questionable advice, such as telling them to stop taking their medicine. If someone else has given them such advice, or they are considering doing something like that, please let one of the leaders know.

5. In public meetings, avoid getting into prayer situations that should be kept private. If a lot of time, intensity or personal interaction is needed, talk to someone about setting up a special session with a prayer team.

6. If the situation is over your head, bring in someone to help, set up a separate session or make a referral (to a pastor, counseling ministry, etc.). This is humility, not failure!

7. Remember, most of us are not professional counselors. Be honest with the people. We are there to pray and seek God together. Don't counsel during prayer. If you do share counsel after a prayer session, share what is on your heart, what has worked for you, etc. Don't give the impression that you are infallible!

8. When prophesying, do not embarrass or shame people. Be cautious about highly directive words pertaining to their business or personal lives. Usually the Lord tells people such things Himself. For example, never tell people whom they should marry!

9. Do not let newcomers who have not been through your training and do not know your guidelines take over the prayer ministry. (They may be free to watch and participate as learners.) We want to teach other people how to minister, but we must constantly ensure the safety of those for whom we pray. You do not want questionable advice and/or methods being employed on unsuspecting people who come for prayer.

10. When you are on a prayer team, if you need prayer for yourself, please seek it out. Be honest if you need it and don't go home without it.

C. Goose Sense

I include this, not only because it is another illustration of a moving "V" (which certainly got my attention when I read it several years after seeing the "V" I spoke of in Chapter Eleven), but also because it is an illustration of the heart for healing, encouragement and comradery God desires us to have.

Lessons from the Geese
by Dr. Robert McNeish
(used by permission)

1.   As each goose flaps its wings it creates an "uplift" for the birds that follows. By flying in a V formation, the whole flock adds 71% greater flying range than if each bird flew alone.

   Lesson: People who share a common direction and sense a community can get where they are going quicker and easier because they are traveling on the thrust of one another.

2.   When a goose falls out of formation, it suddenly feels the drag and resistance of flying alone. It quickly moves back into formation to take advantage of the lifting power of the bird in front of it.

   Lesson: If we have as much sense as a goose we stay in formation with those headed where we want to go. We are willing to accept their help and give our help to others.

3.   When the lead goose tires, it rotates back into the formation and another goose flies to the point position.

Lesson: It pays to take turns doing the hard tasks and sharing leadership. As with geese, people are interdependent on each others skills, capabilities and unique arrangements of gifts, talents or resources.

4. The geese flying in formation honk to encourage those up front to keep up their speed.

Lesson: We need to make sure our honking is encouraging. In groups where there is encouragement, the production is much greater. The power of encouragement is the quality of honking we seek.

5. When a goose gets sick, wounded or shot down, two geese drop out of formation and follow it down to help and protect it. They stay with it until it dies or is able to fly again. Then they launch out with another formation or catch up with the flock.

Lesson: If we have as much sense as geese, we will stand by each other in difficult times as well as when we are strong.

BIBLIOGRAPHY

Brown, Daniel A. with Brian Larson. *The Other Side of Pastoral Ministry – Using Process Leadership to Transform Your Church*. Grand Rapids: Zondervan Publishing House, 1996.

Deere, Jack. *Surprised by the Voice of God – How God Speaks Today Through Prophecies, Dreams and Visions*. Grand Rapids: Zondervan Publishing House, 1996.

Jackson, John Paul. *Developing Your Prophetic Gift*. 4-set CD, North Sutton: Streams Publications.

——. *Needless Casualties of War*. North Sutton: Streams Publications, 1999.

Joyner, Rick. *Leadership, Management and the Five Essentials for Success*. Charlotte: MorningStar Publications, 1990.

——. *The Final Quest*. Charlotte: MorningStar Publications, 1996.

Ladd, George Eldon. *The Gospel of the Kingdom – Scriptural Studies in the Kingdom of God*. Grand Rapids: Eerdmans Publishing Company, 1959, 1988.

Liardon, Roberts. *God's Generals – Why They Succeeded and Why Some Failed*. Tulsa: Albury Publishing, 1996.

MacNutt, Francis. *Healing*. Notre Dame: Ava Maria Press, 1974.

Price, Charles. *The Real Faith*. Plainfield: Logos International, 1940, 1972.

Sjogren, Steve. *Conspiracy of Kindness: A Refreshing Approach to Sharing the Love of Jesus With Others*. Ventura:Vine Books, 1993.

Sheets, Dutch. *Intercessory Prayer*. Ventura: Regal Books, 1996.

Stott, John R.W. *The Message of Ephesians – God's New Society*. Downers Grove: Inter-Varsity Press, 1979.

White, John. *When the Spirit Comes with Power – Signs and Wonders among God's People*. Downers Grove: Inter-Varsity Press, 1988.

Wigram, George V. *The Englishman's Greek Concordance of the New Testament*. Grand Rapids: Zondervan Publishing House, 1970.

Wimber, Carol. *John Wimber, The Way It Was*. London: Hodder & Stoughton, 1999.

Wimber, John with Kevin Springer. *Power Evangelism*. San Francisco: Harper and Row, 1986.

——. *Power Healing*. San Francisco: Harper and Row, 1987.

About the Author

After starting out with a career in scientific research, Randy has pastored (with the Association of Vineyard Churches), taught (at Valparaiso University) and, most importantly, been made part of the royal priesthood of believers! For years he has focused on helping other pastors equip their people to minister—the subject of this book. He has spoken, ministered and taught in various settings, always with an emphasis of having the participants experience the ministry, not just hear about it.

Randy and his wife, Mary, are a part of Church of the Resurrection, an Anglican church in West Chicago, Illinois. They have three daughters, Holly, Becky and Mandy, who are their delights.

---

to contact the author or Byron Arts, see page 2